11 95

DATE DUE

D0194814

DEC 6 198? DEC 27 1999
JAN 16 1984
FEB 20 1984

MAR 29 1984
MAY 21 1984

MAY 22 1986
DEC 14 1986

APR - 4 1987
MAY 9 1987

MAR 22 1992
FEB 22 1996

TWAYNE'S WORLD AUTHORS SERIES
A Survey of the World's Literature

RUSSIA

EDITOR OF THIS VOLUME

Charles Moser, George Washington University

Anton Chekhov

TWAS 568

Anton Chekhov

ANTON CHEKHOV

By Irina Kirk

University of Connecticut, *Storrs*

TWAYNE PUBLISHERS

A DIVISION OF G. K. HALL & CO., BOSTON

Published in 1981 by Twayne Publishers,
A Division of G. K. Hall & Co.
All Rights Reserved

Printed on permanent/durable acid-free paper and bound
in the United States of America

First Printing

Frontispiece drawing by Evan Smith Robinson.

Library of Congress Cataloging in Publication Data

Kirk, Irina.
Anton Chekhov.

(Twayne's world authors series ; TWAS 568 : Russia)
Bibliography: p. 161 - 63
Includes index.
1. Chekhov, Anton Pavlovich, 1860 - 1904—Criticism
and interpretation.
PG3458.Z8K57   891.72'3   80-19110
ISBN 0-8057-6410-0

For William Edgerton

Contents

About the Author

Irina Kirk was born in Manchuria and raised in Shanghai. She received her graduate degree in Comparative and Russian Literature, while working as a teaching assistant. In 1968, she received her Ph.D. from Indiana University. She is now a full professor at the University of Connecticut, Storrs. Her first novel *Born with the Dead* was published in 1963 by Houghton Mifflin. Since then she has published other books including *Dostoevsky and Camus* and *Profiles in Russian Resistance*. Presently, she is working on a novel and a book on the early Dostoevsky.

Preface

"In his amazing objectivity, standing above personal sorrows and joys, he knew everything and saw everything; nothing personal stood in the way of his penetration. He could be kind and generous without loving, affectionate and concerned without attachment. He could be altruistic without counting on gratitude. And in these features that remained always unclear to those who surrounded him is hidden, perhaps, the main riddle of his personality.
—Alexander Kuprin on Chekhov

In surveying the nineteenth-century Russian writers Chekhov seems, if not the most sober, at least far removed from the complexity of Dostoevsky, the personal torments of Tolstoi, and the bizarreness of Gogol. For it is Chekhov's portraits that are most often found on the walls of schools, hospitals, and even psychiatric wards in the Soviet Union today: Chekhov, the calm, compassionate human being, lovable and loving, whose archives contain thousands of letters thanking him for services rendered to friends and strangers.

Yet on closer examination, Chekhov emerges as one of the most enigmatic Russian writers, not only as mystifying as Dostoevsky and as turbulent as Tolstoi, but perhaps even more difficult to define precisely because his complexity is not readily apparent.

Critics have always argued over whether Chekhov was an optimist or a pessimist. Earlier critics such as Aleksander Skabichevsky and Leon Shestov saw him as a gentle singer of despair in whose work "almost every line is a sob." Later critics, following Stanislavsky's declaration that "Chekhov is the greatest optimist of the future I have ever met," reacted against this gloomy view. Ovsyaniko-Kulikovsky, Batushkov, and Chukovsky in Russia, and Robert Payne in the United States (in his preface to Chekhov's anthology of short stories) all maintain with Ivan Bunin that the joy of life was the essence of his nature and that it is reflected in his work.

The argument of whether Chekhov was an optimist or a pessimist implies that he held one or the other monolithic attitude toward life, that he had a definite conception of the world, or what the

Russians call *mirovozzrenie* (world-view). Chekhov possessed nothing so grandiose or so simple. In fact, several Russian critics accused him of lacking any *mirovozzrenie;* and Avram Derman, in defending Chekhov, pointed out that while Chekhov may not have had a world-view, he did have a world-feeling (*miroosh-chushchenie*), and it is this feeling that enabled him to respond spontaneously and impetuously to everything around him. Yet when he sat down to write about people his feelings were replaced by analysis and at times gloom surfaced. This discrepancy may be explained in part by Chekhov's clearheaded objectivity when he wrote, but it also indicated that he was closer perhaps to the twentieth century European existentialist writers than to his Russian intellectual brothers and their predilection for ideologies.

Like the existentialists, Chekhov rejected the notion that self-fulfillment is possible through material acquisitions, fame, or by following a religious or political ideology. While recognizing human aspirations and achievements, Chekhov also knew that attainment does not often result in contentment, and what interested him was precisely the different, hidden nuances of a human psyche reacting to frustration, losses, separation, and insecurity. It was not the desire to dwell on the so-called negative side of life that led Chekhov to concentrate on these subterranean shadows of human nature, but the desire to reach, understand, and portray beyond the appearances.

He began his literary career by parodying the popular fiction, e.g., by rejecting some of the existing genres, thus clearing the way for his own search for artistic values. In his early works there are many satirical sketches ridiculing such human traits as rank-reverence and hypocrisy. Only later, when he was taken seriously by the critics, did he deal with human emotions, sorrow, and ambiguities, and it was on this inconclusive ground that he found his sources. Yet he did not expatiate, in the manner of many Russian writers, on the secret reserves of man's soul. He would rather pinpoint a seemingly insignificant detail or characteristic and through it suddenly reveal the very essence of a person or a situation.

Chekhov is known for the brevity of his expression, for understatement, but within the understatement he was able to give a profound perception of human nature. The brevity served not to narrow but to define the very substance of life.

The main body of this study is a thematic and stylistic treatment of a selection of Chekhov's work, from his early sketches to his final stories and plays, with greater emphasis on the analysis of the stories, since so much has been written on his plays. Rather than place the works of this complex author into neat categories, or explain them by an overriding methodology, I have tried to analyze each work independently, though as part of a continuum. In this manner I hope to suggest the greatness of Chekhov's development as an artist. The man remains a mystery.

IRINA KIRK

Acknowledgments

I wish to acknowledge the editorial assistance of my former student, Nancy Shealy, who helped me with suggestions, revisions, and rewriting.

To the University of Connecticut Research Foundation—my indebtedness for the financial support of this project.

To Professor Herbert Lederer, the former head of the Germanic and Slavic Languages and Literatures department, my gratitude for his encouragement, tolerance, and championship of every cause I espoused which delayed the writing of this book.

And for my children, Misha, Mark, and Katya, without whose enthusiasm and love this book would have been written years ago.

Chronology

1860   January 17. Anton Chekhov born in the city of Taganrog, third son of Pavel Egorovich and Evgeniya Yakovlevna Chekhov.

1867   Begins his education in a Greek Parochial school.

1868   From August 23 attends Taganrog Classical Gimnaziya.

1869   The family moves to the suburbs of Taganrog. Anton attends the Boys' Gynmaziya. Often tends the little grocery store for his father.

1873   October 20. Goes to the theater for the first time, to see *Prekrasnaya Elena* (Beautiful Helen). This marks the beginning of his interest in the theater. Apprenticed to a tailor.

1875   Compiles the handwritten magazine, *Zaika* (Stammerer), for which he writes short, humorous sketches of Taganrog life.

1876   April 23. Pavel Egorovich Chekhov leaves Taganrog clandestinely for Moscow to escape his debtors. Evgeniya Yakovlevna follows in July with her two younger children, Misha and Masha. Anton lives with Selivanov, who purchased the family house for 500 rubles by deceitful means, and tutors Selivanov's nephew in exchange for bed and board.

1877   Writes his first play, *Bezotzovshchina* (Fatherlessness).

1879   After his graduation leaves for Moscow. In September enters the Medical School at Moscow University.

1880   March 9. Publishes his first short story, "The Letter from the Don Landowner Stephan Vladimirovich N. to his Learned Neighbor Dr. Friederick" in the magazine *Strekoza*.

1881   Publishes in magazines, *Alarm Clock* and *Spectator*.

1882   November. Begins to publish in a Petersburg weekly magazine, *Fragments*, and thus becomes a regular contributor.

1884   Graduates from the Moscow University Medical School. In June his first collection of short stories, *Skazki Melpomeny* (Tales of Melpomene), published.

1885   Censorship forbids publication of the story "Sverxshtatny Blyustitel" (A Superfluous Guardian), and the production of a one-act play *Na Bolshoi doroge* (On the Big Road).

1886   Receives a letter from D. Grigorovich in which the older writer asks Chekhov to respect his own talent.

1886   May. Chekhov's collection of short stories, *Pestrye Rasskazy* (Motley Tales), published. Begins collaboration with Suvorin's newspaper, *Novoe Vremya*.

1887   August. Collection of short stories and sketches, *V sumerkakh* (In the Twilight), published.
October. Finishes his play, *Ivanov*.
November 19. First performance of *Ivanov* in Moscow.
December 5. Publishes for the last time as a regular contributor in *Fragments*. This sets him out on a more serious career as a writer.

1888   Works on his povest', "Step' "(Jan. 1 - Feb. 2) which brought him recognition.
May - June. Publication of his book, *Rasskazy* (Tales).
August. Agrees to collaborate in the journal *Epokha*.
October 19. Awarded Pushkin Prize "for the best literary production distinguished by high artistic worth."

1889   Attempts to write a novel.
June. Death of his brother, Nikolai.
Works on *The Wood Demon*.

1890   April 21. Leaves for Sakhalin Island. Arrives on July 11. Remains there until October 13. On return trip visits Hong Kong, Singapore, Ceylon, and Port Said.

1891   March 17. Leaves Petersburg for Vienna with Suvorin. Visits Italy and France. Returns to Russia May 2. Goes to a summer house to work on his book, *Sakhalin Island*.

1892   Takes up residence on country estate, Melikhovo. In a letter to his brother, Aleksandr, about purchasing of Melikhovo, signs himself "Landowner A. Chekhov." Participates in the fight against cholera epidemic.

1893   July. Completes work on *Sakhalin Island*, which is serialized in the last three issues of *Russkaya mysl* in 1893 and the first five months of 1894.

1894   March. Goes to Yalta because of ill health. Returns to Melikhovo May 22. Goes to Taganrog August 24 because of his uncle Mitrofan's illness.

1895   August 8 - 9. First visit to L. Tolstoi at Yasnaya Polyana.
October. Works on his play, *The Seagull*.

1896   October 17. First performance of *The Seagull* in the Aleksandrinsky Theater in Petersburg as a benefit performance for the well-known actress E. I. Levkeeva. Dejected about the play's "failure" though later performances are successful.

1897   March 25. Hospitalized for tuberculosis.

1898   October 12. Pavel Egorovich Chekhov dies in Moscow clinic.

1899   June 16. First letter to Olga Knipper, an actress of the Moscow Art Theater.

1900   January 8. Selected as an honorary member of the Academy of Sciences in the field of literature.

1901   January 31. First performance of *Three Sisters* at the Moscow Art Theater.

        May 25. Marries Olga Knipper in Moscow. They leave for Ufim Province.

1902   August 25. Refuses honorary membership in the Academy of Sciences because of Gorky's expulsion from it.

1903   February. Begins work on *The Cherry Orchard*. Health deteriorates.

        December. Complete works of Chekhov in 16 volumes (second edition) published by A. F. Marx.

1904   January 17. First performance of *The Cherry Orchard* at Moscow Art Theater and celebration of Chekhov's 25th anniversary of literary work.

        June 3. Chekhov and Olga Knipper leave for Badenweiler because of his increasingly bad health.

        July 2. Dies at 3 a.m.

        July 9. Funeral in Moscow at the Novodevichy Cemetery.

CHAPTER 1

Life

"A writer needs maturity and a feeling of personal freedom," wrote Chekhov at the age of 28 "and that feeling began to burn in me only recently."[1] He then proposed a subject for a story in obvious reference to his own youth and childhood.

. . . how a young man, the son of a serf, a former grocery boy, chorister, high school lad and university student, who was brought up to respect rank, to kiss priests' hands, to revere other people's ideas, to give thanks for every morsel of bread, who was whipped many times, who without rubbers traipsed from pupil to pupil, who used his fists and tormented animals, who was fond of dining with rich relatives, who was hypocritical in his dealings with God and men gratuitously, out of the mere consciousness of his insignificance—write how this youth squeezes the slave out of himself drop by drop, and how, waking up one fine morning, he feels that in his veins flows no longer the blood of a slave but that of a real man. . .[2]

The determination to squeeze the slave out of himself must have been conceived back in Taganrog, where he was born and where his ill-tempered father (himself the son of a slave) kept a small grocery story in which Anton Chekhov often worked as a child. Part of his father's bad disposition must have come from frustration, for he was not without talent himself and liked to paint, play the violin, and took active part in the church choir where Anton had to sing. Apparently the artistic streak in the nature of Pavel Chekhov was stronger than his business sense; he ended up with only the debts and had to escape his creditors by sneaking off to Moscow.

Chekhov's mother, left without any support, took in a boarder, G. P. Selivanov, an employee of the civil court, who offered to help the family with the suit against Pavel Egorovich. Instead, Selivanov paid five hundred rubles (the original loan) and transferred the deed on the house to himself. The furniture was auctioned to pay off the interest on the loan. Evgeniya Chekhova, taking her son

17

Misha and her daughter Masha, followed her husband to Moscow, leaving Anton with Selivanov, in the role of a tutor to Selivanov's nephew. Anton, who was sixteen at the time, spent the next three years in the house that no longer belonged to his family, trying to make a living by doing odd jobs and tutoring.

Though Chekhov was initiated into poverty and humilitation early in life, there were lighter moments in his youth, and in those moments he used to entertain his friends by mimicking the members of local society. This ability to see the comic in life, to grasp and imitate the essence of another, was probably the source of a writer whose tragic sense of life was always tempered by simultaneous awareness of the ridiculous.

Yet this cognizance of the absurd in human nature did not rob the young Chekhov of compassion nor of a desire to be of service as a healer. His decision to become a medical doctor probably dates to the summer of 1875 when he fell ill with peritonitis and was cared for by Dr. Schrempf. The school physician must have found an interested and receptive listener in his patient for he shared with Chekhov his own memories of being a medical student at the University of Dorpat. References to the possibility of entering a medical school either in Moscow or abroad begin to appear in Chekhov's letters as he neared his graduation from Taganrog High School. Following his graduation and after spending most of the summer in Taganrog, Chekhov finally left for Moscow on August 6, 1879, together with his two classmates, V. I. Zembulatov and D. T. Saveliev, who were also planning to enter medical school.

For many, the years spent in a university are a prolonging of a blissful state of being on the threshold of life—the passing into adulthood with its new privileges, but with more serious responsibilities still lying beyond. For Anton Chekhov, his entrance into the medical school of Moscow University was also the assuming of responsibility for his large family. His father, who earned thirty rubles a month, lived at the place of his work and only visited his wife and children on Sundays. The family, accustomed to the stern authority of the father, felt a void in his absence, and by a mutual, unspoken consent, this void was filled by Anton. In jest, his brother, Aleksandr, called him "Father Antosha"; once again a burden had a comic aspect.

"Father Antosha" did not participate in the social or political activities of the Moscow University students, even though the assassination of Tsar Aleksandr II on March 1, 1881, stirred a great deal of unrest among the students. Chekhov's instinct, always on guard against herd mentality, was to distrust ideologies and in particular the ideologies based on theories removed from personal experience. Besides, his responsibilities for his family left him little time from studying medicine and thinking up ways in which to supplement his income from tutoring.

The oldest brother, Aleksandr, who chose to be poor, lived alone in a rented room away from the family. He earned a small income by writing for humorous magazines, such as *Alarm Clock* or *Dragonfly*, and urged Anton to submit his writing to the same publications. He tried, but without success. Then on January 13, 1880, Anton finally found in the section called "Letter Box of the Weekly," of *Dragonfly* (where comments were printed to would-be writers): "Not bad at all. Will print what was sent. Our blessings for your future efforts." It was in reference to his story, "A Letter from the Don Landowner Stephan Vladimirovich N., to his Learned Neighbor Dr. Friederick." The story was published in the March issue of 1880, thus launching Chekhov on his literary career.

In October of 1882 Chekhov was introduced to N. A. Leikin, publisher and editor of a Petersburg weekly magazine, *Fragments*. Leikin expressed interest in Chekhov's work and asked him to send in some of his stories. In November Chekhov's first story was published in *Fragments* and he soon became a regular contributor to the magazine.

On the part of Leikin, the arrangement with Chekhov was good business. Not only did Chekhov work fast, but he lacked any vanity and pretensions. He wrote under a pseudonym, Antosha Chekhonte, and at times he used others such as A Man without a Spleen, A Physician without Patients, Brother of my Brother. The only difficulty that Leikin encountered with Chekhov was when he tried to dictate the form or content of his stories. This occurred whenever the mood of a story would shift from the purely light-humorous to even slightly philosophical. And though Leikin himself missed the process of development and growth of a writer contributing to his own magazine, others did not; so that when, in the end of 1885, Chekhov traveled to Petersburg for the first time, at the invitation of Leikin, he was surprised to find himself quite well known. On the advice of the novelist Dmitry Grigorovich, A. S. Suvorin, the owner of the most influential newspaper, *Novoe Vremya (New Times)*, invited Chekhov to contribute his longer works to the daily. In February, 1886, Chekhov's tale, *The Re-*

quiem, was published in *Novoe Vremya,* marking the beginning of his long association with Suvorin. Chekhov was immensely pleased with this new arrangement and wrote Suvorin (Feb. 21, 1886) ". . . I've been writing for six years, but you are the first person who has taken the trouble to advise a cut and to motivate it."[3]

Thanks to his improving income, Chekhov was able to rent a much better house, near the center of Moscow, on Sadovaya Kudrinskaya Street. As always he was concerned about improving the living conditions of his family, and in this new house there was an extra room where Chekhov could write and see patients. The family began to realize now that Chekhov's writing was not only the means for an extra income, but an expression of a significant talent. But, as pleased as his mother was with the growing fame of her son, she did not stop lamenting the fact that he was still a bachelor and had not heeded her advice to marry a rich merchant's daughter. His brothers admired him, and his sister, Masha, in her reverence, was prepared to place herself at his service. In fact, some years later, Masha refused a marriage proposal from a man she loved in order to remain with her brother.

But, despite all this, Chekhov suffered from a sense of dissatisfaction with himself which is reflected in his letters as well as in his desire to revisit the place of his birth, "so that I won't dry up"[4] (Feb. 10, 1887). In April, 1887, he left Moscow for Taganrog, from where he planned to travel to the Don Steppe. His instinct was correct; the journey across the vast expanses of a changeable and elusive landscape must have been stirring and it resulted later (1888) in the creation of Chekhov's most poetic story, "The Steppe."

In 1888 Chekhov's attention turned to playwriting and he worked on *The Wood Demon* which he finished in October, 1889. Playwriting was not a new genre for Chekhov; in 1887 he wrote *Ivanov* and it was successfully performed in Moscow on November 19 of that year. Thus he must have been unprepared when the Committee of the Alexandrinsky Theater rejected *The Wood Demon* and A. P. Lensky, one of the great actors, wrote to advise Chekhov to stick to writing stories. In his reply Chekhov agreed with Lensky that he obviously had no talent for the theater. But in November the actor, N. N. Solovtsov, decided to stage it at the Moscow Abramov Theater. Though Chekhov revised it, *The Wood Demon,* which opened on December 27, was castigated by the critics. Several years later, after he had mastered the drama form,

The Wood Demon served him as raw material for one of his finest plays, *Uncle Vanya*.

But the initial failure of *The Wood Demon* must have contributed to the spiritual crisis that was apparently building up as Chekhov approached the critical age of thirty. On May 4 he wrote to Suvorin, ". . . over the past two years, and for no earthly reason, I've grown sick of seeing my work in print, have become indifferent to reviews, to talks on literature, to slander, successes, failure, big fees—in fact, I've turned into an utter fool. There is a sort of stagnation in my soul. I explain it by the stagnation in my personal life."[5]

To dispel the stagnation in his soul Chekhov chose one of the solutions that is usually more effective than any self-concern, that of concern for others. He decided on an arduous and difficult journey to Sakhalin Island, to investigate conditions for the inmates of the penal colony on that far away Pacific island.

He went about it in a rather scholarly fashion, traveling to Petersburg for the purpose of collecting written material on the subject and in hopes of obtaining some sort of official letter that would facilitate his work on Sakhalin. Sister Masha and brother Aleksandr were recruited to do more reading and to compile a bibliography, and Chekhov himself studied everything from the weather, to the soil conditions, to the price of coal. Finally, on April 21, 1890, the train pulled out from the Yaroslav station in Moscow, taking Chekhov on his long journey to Sakhalin. He traveled by rail, by steamers, by horses, in all kinds of wicked weather, over rugged roads and rough waters. He arrived at Irkutsk on June 4, and took a rest there before resuming his journey on June 11. The trip over the spectacular Lake Baikal elicited some very lyrical passages in Chekhov's letters to his mother and sister, and he was "giddy with ecstasy" about the scenery in the Amur region. After changing from the river steamer to another river boat, to the liner *Baikal,* and crossing the Gulf of Tatary, Chekhov arrived at Sakhalin on July 11 and went to Alexandrovsk, the prison center of the island, and its main town.

Chekhov spent three months on Sakhalin. He interviewed the convicts, took a census of the entire population, and visited virtually every inhabitant. After two months he wrote to Suvorin, "I don't know what will come of it, but I've done not a little. It is enough for three dissertations. I got up each day at 5 a.m., went to bed late, and all my days were spent in a great state of tension from the thought that there is so much left to be done."[6] (September 11,

1890). When he left Sakhalin on October 13, Chekhov took a different route home which must have satisfied his everlasting wanderlust. He stopped in Hong Kong, Singapore, Colombo, and Ceylon. But it also must have been rather taxing, for when he got back to Moscow he was quite ill.

However, that did not deter him from another trip abroad, and three months later, on March 17, 1891, he joined Suvorin and his son for a trip to Europe. After the rigors of Siberia and Sakhalin, the elegance of Vienna, the magnificence of Venice, Rome, and Florence overwhelmed him. To his brother, he wrote that he longed to remain there forever. And to his sister, in explaining why he would live in the land of Michelangelo and Leonardo, he said, "For Italy, apart from its natural scenery and warmth, is the only country in which one feels convinced that art is really supreme over everything, and that conviction gives one courage"[7] (Apr. 1, 1891). But Paris, for all its charm, made him nostalgic for his family, and on May 2 he returned to Russia.

The journey to Sakhalin Island dispelled the stagnation in Chekhov's soul and made him reexamine his own situation in regard to literature and medicine. "If I'm a doctor, I ought to have patients and a hospital," he wrote to Suvorin on October 19, 1891; "if I am a literary man, then I ought to live among people instead of on Malaya Dmitrovka with a mongoose. I need a bit of social and political life, even though it be a small bit, but this life within four walls, without nature and people, without a country, without health or appetite—this isn't life. . . ."[8]

What he apparently needed or longed for was a place of his own, in the country, where he could write and have nature and people and be away from Moscow. He asked his brother and sister to look for a place in the country for him. What they found was an estate, Melikhovo, two and a half hours from Moscow, and Chekhov decided to buy it before he had even a chance to see it. On March 5 he moved into his own home. "My impressions and state of mind are wonderful, such as they have not been in a long time," he wrote on that day to his brother. He was a landowner now; for the son of a serf it must have had an especially poignant significance.

He planted cherry and apple trees in the orchard, spent hours improving the estate and filling its grounds with flowers. For Chekhov, Melikhovo was not only a property to be owned, it afforded him the opportunity to satisfy his craving for beauty and to give his family a home. By the time the second summer came around, Melikhovo became the gathering place for relatives, friends, acquaintances, even strangers. Chekhov also practiced medicine in Melikhovo, riding over all sorts of non-roads to visit the sick villagers, and accepted the trusteeship of the Talezh village school.

In August, 1895, I. I. Gorbunov-Posadov, a friend of Lev Tolstoi, was visiting Melikhovo on his way to Yasnaya Polyana, so Chekhov took the opportunity to meet the writer whom he admired. Chekhov spent August 8 and 9 with Tolstoi and this first visit left a most favorable impression on both writers. Later Chekhov would acquire a skeptical attitude toward Tolstoi's wisdom and his subordination of artistic autonomy to moralizing. But for some time after the visit he remained under the spell of the great novelist.

When Chekhov wrote to Suvorin about the stagnation of his personal life, he probably meant the lack of romantic attachment. He had a devoted family, enjoyed their love and respect, yet he seemed to have purposely avoided any serious involvement with a woman. According to Lydia Avilova, a married woman who aspired to become a writer, Chekhov was in love with her after they first met in 1889. However, as Ernest J. Simmons has documented in his biography on Chekhov, it was most probably Avilova's projection that made her imagine this affection. It seems that he was far more predisposed toward Lidiya Mizinova, "the beautiful Lika," as he called her, a young school teacher whom Masha introduced into the household in 1889. On the way to Sakhalin, from Siberia, Chekhov wrote his mother that he must be in love with Lika because he dreamed about her one night; and though the letter was in his usual joking tone, whenever he spoke of intimate feelings, there were reasons to suspect that there was some truth to the notion.

"The beautiful Lika," in turn was apparently quite deeply in love with Chekhov, and in the middle of May, 1891, she came to visit him at the rented dacha in Aleksin. His behavior toward her was highly ambivalent as must have been his emotions. On the one hand, he discouraged any expression of feeling from her and kept assuring her that he would never marry. On the other hand, he wrote her mock love letters with mock proposals: "I love you passionately, like a tiger, and offer you my hand"[9] (July, 1891).

When Chekhov acquired the Melikhovo estate, Lika was a frequent visitor there, too, and whenever he went to Moscow he always made an effort to see her. He continued to write her most endearing letters, especially during 1892. But at the end of her visits to Melikhovo in 1893, Lika realized that something in him was either frightened or leery of marriage. She wrote him a candid letter in which she expressed her feelings, saying that she realized his behavior toward her was "condescending and indifferent." She began seeing I. N. Potapenko, a writer whom she met at Melikhovo during that year. In 1894, Potapenko and Lika went to Europe together even though Potapenko had a wife.

Because Chekhov was extremely reticent about his private life and shared his thoughts on that subject with no one, it is difficult for his biographers to reconstruct his relationship with women. From what little evidence we have it is possible that he had difficulties both in letting Lika go and in allowing himself to get involved. On September 14, he left for Europe once again, without informing anyone at home, and four days later he wrote Lika, who was in Switzerland, after Potapenko had returned to Russia, leaving her pregnant and depressed. She wrote back asking Chekhov to come and see her, adding her conviction that he would not cast a stone at her because "It seems to me that you were always indifferent to people, to their inadequacies and weaknesses."[10]

Whether because of a sense of guilt, jealousy, or because he was hurt by her words accusing him of indifference, Chekhov decided against going to Switzerland and returned to Russia via Paris. Lika had her baby, but after she returned to Russia the child died. Whatever distress it all caused him, Chekhov reached for the therapy available to a writer; he fictionalized the experience in his play *The Seagull*. And after the failure of *The Seagull* at its first performance, he left for Melikhovo and wrote Masha to come and bring Lika with her.

Whenever he was abroad he wrote Lika, and when he did not hear from her, Chekhov asked his sister for news about Lika. Several times he had asked her to join him for different trips and, in short, it seemed that he preferred her company to that of any other woman he knew. And yet he was never able to feel the kind of deep attachment that she felt for him.

In October he began working on *The Seagull*. When he finished, he sent it to Suvorin and read it to friends and members of his family at Melikhovo. Suvorin, as well as those present at the reading, noted the resemblance between Chekhov's characters and Lika and Potapenko. Chekhov was not pleased with that. He was either unaware himself of how close this resemblance was or else he thought that his disguises were less transparent. He set out to revise it.

The Seagull opened on October 17, 1896, as a benefit for the well-known comic actress E. I. Levkeeva, at the Alexandrinsky Theater in Petersburg. Levkeeva's audience, which filled the theater expecting to see its favorable actress perform her usual comic routine, could not fathom what was happening on stage. Nor was that audience reluctant to express its indignation and disappointment. The expression had gotten so shrill that Chekhov left his seat after the second act, stayed backstage to the end of the performance, and then walked the streets alone in the night.

The next day he wrote to Suvorin, "I shall never forget yesterday evening, but still I slept well, and am setting off in a very tolerable good humor. I am not going to produce the play in Moscow. I shall *never* either write plays or have them acted"[11] (Oct. 18, 1896). That day he left for Melikhovo. Though the second, third, fourth, and fifth performances of *The Seagull* were successful, and Chekhov's friends wrote him about its triumph, Chekhov still felt vexed and ashamed. Several months later, the trauma had apparently caught up with Chekhov and manifested itself in a grave physical illness. He had in fact mentioned ill health the day after he arrived in Melikhovo. For the next few months he continued to feel unwell, and on March 21 he began to spit blood. Nevertheless, the next morning he went to Moscow. That evening, during dinner with Suvorin, he had another bleeding spell, and on March 25 he was taken to Ostroumov Clinic. Three days later, Lev Tolstoi came to visit Chekhov and lectured him on immortality and on the degeneration of art. After two and a half weeks at the clinic he was discharged and went to Melikhovo.

His health continued to be precarious, and at the end of August his doctors advised him to escape the coming cold by going abroad. He left for Biarritz on August 31, 1897. He enjoyed the sun and the "stamp of civilization," and if he had any homesickness it expressed itself only by the voluminous correspondence with all his friends in Russia. Mindful of not worrying his family, he gave careful and often understated accounts of his condition. During October and November he wrote only three short stories, "The Pecheng," "At Home," and "In the Cart."

In November, 1897, while Chekhov was staying in Nice, the French press began once again to write about Captain Alfred Dreyfus, condemned in 1894 to life imprisonment as an alleged spy for Germany. Chekhov followed all the accounts with great interest, and when Émile Zola's famous letter, *J'accuse*, appeared on January

13, he became even more involved in the case, siding with those who believed Dreyfus was framed. Suvorin, however, remained with those who did not believe Dreyfus was innocent, and his *New Times* continued the campaign against Dreyfus with definite anti-Semitic undertones. At first there was a sharp disagreement between Chekhov and Suvorin; then Chekhov, having decided that it would be more sensible to make Suvorin understand the case better, wrote him a long letter explaining all the new evidence. Suvorin's answer did not survive, but whatever he personally thought, the *New Times* continued to be against Zola, and soon the correspondence between Suvorin and Chekhov ceased.

It resumed only in April, when Suvorin wrote that he was going to be in Paris and Chekhov replied by saying he would meet him there. "I've accumulated a mass of all kinds of things—both feelings and thoughts—to discuss with you."[12] (Apr. 6, 1898). They did meet in Paris and spent a lot of time together. On the surface the quarrel over the Dreyfus affair seemed to have been patched up, but the friendship never again resumed its former intimate character. Though they planned to return to Russia together, Chekhov left Paris on May 2 alone.

During that summer also Nemirovich-Danchenko and Konstantin Stanislavski, the directors of the newly established Moscow Art Theater, decided to stage *The Seagull*. Having at first refused to give his permission, Chekhov finally succumbed to Nemirovich-Danchenko's persuasive powers. On September 9, 1898, Chekhov appeared at the rehearsal where he met Olga Leonardovna Knipper, the young actress who was playing the role of Arkadina. On September 14 he attended a rehearsal of A. Tolsoi's play, *Tsar Fedor*, in which Olga played Irina. Nearly a month later he wrote to Suvorin, "In my opinion Irina was splendid. Her voice, her nobility, her sincerity was so superb that I felt choked with emotion . . . If I had remained in Moscow I would have fallen in love with this Irina"[13] (Oct. 8, 1898).

Chekhov wished to remain in Moscow, but another illness forced him to leave for a warmer climate, this time Yalta. He rented two rooms in a private home and was soon involved in the Town Council, Red Cross, and began to campaign in the press for starving children in Samara. On October 14, he received the news of his father's death at Melikhovo. He wrote to Masha, "It seems to me that with father's death life won't be the same at Melikhovo"[14] (Oct. 14, 1898). And indeed he began to plan the sale of Melikhovo and a move to Yalta. He borrowed five thousand rubles from Suvorin against his royalties to buy some land in Autka, near Yalta, and a bank advanced him the money to build a house.

On December 17, Chekhov's thoughts were in Moscow, for on that day his *Seagull* was to open at the Art Theater. It was a significant day not only for Chekhov, but for Stanislavsky, Nemirovich-Danchenko, and the entire Moscow Art Theater. The performance was a colossal success, and Nemirovich-Danchenko wired Chekhov, "With wonderful unanimity all newspapers acclaim success of *The Seagull* as brilliant, tumultuous, enormous. For our theater success of *The Seagull* surpasses success of Fyodor."[15] Chekhov answered, "Convey to all: infinite thanks with all my soul. I'm confined to Yalta, like Dreyfus on Devil's Island. I grieve that I'm not with you. Your telegram made me well and happy."[16]

Chekhov returned to Moscow on April 12, 1899, and on April 18, Easter Sunday, he went to visit Olga Knipper. In the first week of May, Olga came to visit him at Melikhovo. When she left for her vacation in the Caucasus it was with an understanding that they would soon take a trip together. And on July 18, they met in Novosibirsk and took a boat to Yalta. They spent two weeks in Yalta and then returned to Moscow together. However, for all his desire to remain in Moscow, his deteriorating health once more drove Chekhov back to Yalta.

On January 17, 1900, while Chekhov was feeling ill at Yalta, his friends at Masha's Moscow apartment, together with Olga Knipper and Lika Mizinova, celebrated Chekhov's fortieth birthday and his election to the Academy of Science. It was difficult for Chekhov to be isolated now that the stagnation was gone from his personal and professional life. On February 10, he wrote Olga, "I have been uprooted from my native soil. My life is incomplete. I don't drink, although I like drinking. I like it when it's noisy but I don't hear any noise. In a word, I now endure the condition of a transplanted tree which hesitates between taking root and starting to wither away"[17] (Feb. 10, 1900).

But in the spring the Moscow Art Theater brought *Uncle Vanya* and *The Seagull* to Yalta for a tour, and the success of the plays as well as the reunion with all his friends gave Chekhov a great boost. At the beginning of July, Olga Knipper returned to Yalta to spend her vacation with Chekhov. Neither Olga nor Chekhov wanted any intrusion of their time together that summer; there is nothing in her memoirs about it, and Chekhov did not even mention her name in any of his letters of that period. The only indication of the developing intimacy is in the changed tone of correspondence between them following Olga's return to Moscow. His own nostalgia was perhaps best expressed in that he began working in earnest on a new play, *Three Sisters*. The play was finished on October 16 and a few days later Chekhov was in Moscow reading *Three Sisters* to the members of the Moscow Art Theater.

Chekhov and Olga Knipper were married on May 25, 1901. To the very end Chekhov remained extremely secretive, and with his well-known distaste for jubilees, speeches, and champagne toasts, he was determined to keep the ceremony as intimate as possible.

The telegram to his mother at Yalta simply read, "Dear mama, your blessings, I'm married. Everything will remain as before. I'm off to take a kumiss treatment."

The person who was most affected by his marriage was his sister Masha. As she wrote to Ivan Bunin, she was "broken up" over the marriage. Her lifetime devotion to her brother seemed useless now that he had no need of her. Although he wrote that everything would remain as before, the bond between them was, if not broken, at least lacerated. But it must have been equally difficult for Olga to live in the shadow of that devotion. Neither she nor Chekhov could devote the necessary energy to build the marriage: Chekhov, because of his health, had to spend a lot of time in Yalta; Olga, because of her career, had to live in Moscow.

Though *Three Sisters* enjoyed a tremendous success when it was performed in Petersburg in March, 1902, Olga's letters reveal her doubts about having to be away from her husband at the time of his need for her. It also, perhaps, took away something they both wanted very much. On March 31, she wrote Chekhov that she had had a miscarriage. Neither had realized that she was pregnant when Olga had to leave Yalta for Petersburg to resume her work in the theater. Olga was brought on a stretcher to Yalta after her ten-day stay in a Moscow hospital and for the next two months Chekhov tended to her, until he himself was exhausted and spent.

This interrupted his work on *The Cherry Orchard* which he conceived in January, 1902. All of that year Chekhov attempted to work on his new play, but his strength diminished, and it was exceedingly difficult for him to work. On October 12, when the play was finally finished, it was a victory over his devastation by disease. The telegrams that Stanislavsky and Nemirovich-Danchenko sent upon reading *The Cherry Orchard* confirmed that victory. The opening night was scheduled for January 17, 1904, Chekhov's forty-fourth birthday.

But, for all his elation on reading *The Cherry Orchard,* Stanislavsky did not understand Chekhov's intention for it to be a comedy, and he proceeded to direct it as a drama. After seeing the reheasals Chekhov was convinced that the play would fail. So was Stanislavsky. Therefore, he decided to make the night of the premiere the celebration of Chekhov's twenty-fifth anniversary as an author.

Chekhov, suspicious of all this, refused to attend the opening night and came to the theater only after the third act, upon receiving a note that the actors wanted to see him. He was brought on stage before the audience and the actors, and the kind of celebration began that he despised most of all. Speeches were made, telegrams read, flowers showered on the author, who, for all his distaste for such activities, must have been bewildered at such exaltation.

A month later he left for Yalta planning to return to Moscow in May. On his way back to Moscow, Chekhov became very sick and Olga called in her family doctor, Taube, who decided that as soon as it was possible for Chekhov to travel, he should go to Germany to be treated by a specialist in tuberculosis. When on June 2, the day before he and Olga left for Badenweiler, Chekhov saw his friend, the writer N. Teleshov, he told him, "Tomorrow I leave. Goodbye. I'm going to croak" (Okolevat' edu).

Travel, as always, revived him for a little while. From Villa Friederike, a private pension where they settled, Chekhov wrote home that he was getting well "by leaps and bounds." He was under the care of the local physician, Dr. Schwohrer. On June 29 he had an attack that weakened his heart considerably, and the next day the attack occurred again. On June 30 he requested money from a Berlin bank with instructions that the money should be sent to his wife's name. To her question about these instructions, he replied, "Well, you know, just in case."

On July 1, he felt better toward the evening and he asked Olga to go take a walk in the park. When she returned, he began making up a funny story the setting of which was a health resort. "After the anxiety of the previous days," says Olga in her memoirs, "I sat curled up on the couch and laughed from the bottom of my soul" (*ot dushi smejalas'*).[18]

After a while Chekhov fell asleep but woke up again shortly after midnight in delirium, ". . . talked about some sailor, asked about the Japanese," writes Olga, and then surprised her by requesting that a doctor be called. When she tried to put an ice pack on his heart, he smiled sadly and told her, "On an empty heart ice should not be placed." When Dr. Schwohrer arrived at two in the morning, Chekhov told the German physician, "Ich sterbe." The doctor ordered a new oxygen tank, but Chekhov stopped him. "There is no longer a need. I'll be dead before they would bring it."

Dr. Schwohrer then ordered champagne. Chekhov took a glass, turned to Olga, and said, "It's been a long time since I drank champagne." He drained the glass, quietly laid down on his left side, and closed his eyes.

His body was shipped back to Russia for the burial. The train car in which the coffin was placed bore a sign on the outside, "Fresh Oysters." Some of his friends were outraged that the body of their beloved writer was thus transported to his own country. Chekhov, one feels, would have been delighted with the irony and that final touch of the absurd.

CHAPTER 2

Early Chekhov

M OST critics agree that Chekhov's early works were determined in large part by the kind of journals that existed in
Russia at the time and the demands they placed on the writer.
These journals, which flourished in response to a new phenomenon,
the mass reader, were light humor magazines such as *Entertain-
ment, Fragments, Dragonfly, Observer,* and *Alarm Clock.* As the
titles suggest, these publications thrived on a specific genre of
writing: witty, punch-line anecdotes and stories about everyday
people with whom the mass reader could easily identify. Writing for
these journals could not have been exactly beneficial for a serious
writer in the process of development. Yet, insignificant as the early
stories may be in themselves, they indicate quite clearly some of the
thematic and stylistic interests that would occupy Chekhov for the
rest of his life.

Unlike most beginning authors, Chekhov did not rely heavily
upon introspective observations of his own personality for creating
his characters. On the contrary, Chekhov's characters are drawn
from everyday people, and their speech and actions associate them
with certain recognizable social types. Thus, in his first published
story, "A letter from the Don Landowner Stephan Vladimirovich
N., to his Learned Neighbor Dr. Friederick," Chekhov employs the
persona and the *skaz* (language) of a pompous, self-satisfied, ignorant landowner, who is trying to make the acquaintance of his
scholarly neighbor, a certain Dr. Friederich:

Permit me, esteemed neighbor, to introduce myself to you, if only through
these ancient hieroglyphics permit me to mentally shake your learned hand
and to welcome you upon your arrival from St. Petersburg into our un-
worthy continent, inhabited by peasants and rural population: by the ple-
bian element . . . It is said that you published a lot of books while sitting
with tubes, thermometers, and a heap of foreign books with fascinating il-

lustrations . . . . I am terribly devoted to science. . . . Every discovery torments me like a nail in the back. . . . (I, 143).

Even in this first story Chekhov refrains from direct authorial intrusion. The narrator is left to reveal himself and stand before the reader's judgment. The rather heavy-handed irony lies in the discrepancy between the subject of the letter (knowledge and science) and the crude use of language: incongruous similes, misspelled words, and faulty sentences—all of which reveal the narrator's primitive mentality.

Chekhov used the device of self-characterization again in his short sketch "Nadenka N's Homework," which appeared in *Dragonfly* on June 5, 1880. This sketch is an excellent example of the young writer's ability to portray a person and his environment within just a few sentences. In her homework Nadenka has to give examples for different grammatical rules. Through such sentences as : "Papa did not receive a promotion, so he got angry and resigned because of family circumstances," or "Parents marry off their daughters to military men who possess capital and their own houses," Nadenka reveals not only her own limitations, but also the mediocrity of her environment.

Many of Chekhov's earliest works were parodies of literary genres popular at the time. "What One Meets Most Often in Novels, Short Stories and So On" is a direct listing of such items as "Countesses with traces of their former beauty . . . fair-haired heroes . . . impoverished noblemen . . . inflammation of the brain." "My Jubilee" is a parody of jubilee speeches: an unpublished writer is celebrating a three-year anniversary of rejection slips, and he makes a toast to the end of a literary career that had never begun. In "A Thousand and One Passions" Chekhov parodies the so-called "boulevard roman" and the romantic novels imitating Victor Hugo, to whom the story is dedicated.

As much as he was interested in parodies, however, Chekhov was not above using the existing genres himself. "For the Apples" (August 17, 1880) is written in a manner very similar to the "accusatory naturalism" of Zola and many Russian writers of the time. The story shows the helplessness of two peasants before the sadistic brutality of an old landowner. While walking around his grounds, Trifon Semenovich comes upon a young couple eating apples in his orchard. After some deliberately sweet words such as "How is your health, darlings?" he forces them to beat each other while he watches.

In June of 1882, as a result of a bet with A. D. Kurepin, the editor of *Alarm Clock*, Chekhov began a novel, *The Unnecessary Victory*. He maintained that he could write a novel set in a foreign country "no worse than those of the popular foreign writers."[2] *The Unnecessary Victory* was serialized in nine issues of *Alarm Clock* and may actually have been longer had the editor not finally insisted that Chekhov leave this particular genre to others, and go back to writing short stories.

Critics usually consider *The Unnecessary Victory* an imitation of the works of Jokai Mor, a Hungarian novelist popular at the time. Some readers actually believed that it came from Mor's pen, since it depicted the Hungarian aristocracy in Paris. Yet however intentionally imitative *The Unnecessary Victory* may have been, at the same time it contains some of the themes and symbols that would later preoccupy Chekhov. Shattered dreams in particular play an important role in the novel. In his youth the protagonist, Baron von Zainitza, had shown great potential. But ultimately he becomes disillusioned with life, tired of working, and gradually degenerates into a drunken vagabond. The expectations of a young girl named Ilka are also frustrated; this is foreshadowed by a wounded bird. This theme is embodied in an allegory first told to the young baron by his nurse: A fairy lives inside a tulip and spends all her time taking care of various insects. A black spider comes and offers her a choice of marriage to him or death. The insects pledge to protect the good fairy, but when the spider returns they only stand and watch her die.

Even more characteristic of the later Chekhov is "Belated Blossoms," which was serialized in *Common Sense* beginning October 10, 1882. This story is perhaps the most thematically significant of the early works. It details the disintegration of the Priklonsky family, whose members included an old princess, a young and idealistic daughter, Marusya, and a weak and degenerate son, Egorushka. The two women must watch helplessly as Egorushka hastens the loss of their estate by his drinking and carousing. Contrasted with this situation is the growing fame and fortune of Dr. Toporkov, a former serf in the Priklonsky household. Toporkov had once possessed humanistic dreams, but in time the main interest of his life became the accumulation of "rubles, rugs and expensive watches." Marusya, however, mistakes the doctor's taciturn and abrupt manner for depth of character, and she nurses a secret love for him for many years. Finally, just before her death she confesses her feelings for him, causing Toporkov to recognize that he has lived with false values. He tries to save her life, but it is too late. Filled with remorse, he undertakes the support of Egorushka.

Critics often see Chekhov's "work as salvation" philosophy as a later develoment; however, this issue receives its first treatment in "Belated Blossoms." He contrasts the industrious, persevering, constantly active Dr. Toporkov with the degenerate nobility. At first glance Toporkov seems definitely to gain by the contrast, but in the final analysis his existence also proves useless. Chekhov seems to be saying here that if an active life lacks elevating meaning, it is just as sterile as the life of a man who does nothing.

Stylistically, the work is quite crude. The story is drawn out, sentimental, and lacking in subtlety. The characters are undeveloped, and they often act in an unmotivated manner. The work does, however, evoke a certain mood, creating a world filled with impotent lives, wasted emotions, and the absence of communication.

These early stories and sketches are interesting for the purpose of tracing Chekhov's literary beginning, but they have little inherent artistic value. Chekhov himself was aware of their weaknesses, and included none of them in his *Collected Works* in 1889. Yet for all their stylistic awkwardness, they do not give the impression of a naive, untutored, and unsophisticated young writer, eager for self-expression and searching for the meaning of life. On the contrary, they are the products of an observant mind with an insight and perception that usually come from the experience of a middle-aged man. Almost every biographer of Chekhov begins with the author's own words: "In childhood I had no childhood." These stories are evidence that he had no youth either.

For the next three years (1883 - 85) Chekhov's best work dealt with the phenomenon known in Russian as *chinopochitanie*, meaning rank-reverence. He directed his satire particularly at the officials of the Russian Civil Service, although he was not interested in attacking the bureaucracy itself so much as in showing the particular obsequious mentality that it created.

The hero of "Death of a Government Clerk" (1883), Ivan Dmitrich Chervyakov, is attending an opera performance "thinking himself the most blessed among mortals," when he suddenly sneezes and accidentally sprays the man in front of him. This gentleman turns out to be a high official in the civil service. Chervyakov, only a clerk and overwhelmed by the magnitude of his deed, immediately renders a dramatic apology. The general dismisses him indifferently, but the clerk is sure that he must somehow make amends. Throughout the story he tries to expiate his crime. The general finally loses his temper, throwing the clerk out of his office. Chervyakov returns home emotionally shattered, lies down, and dies.

The idea for "Death of a Government Clerk" was given to Chekhov by V. Begichev, a famous director of the Moscow Theatre, who apparently witnessed a similar incident in the Bolshoi Theatre. The story is built on contrast: between the insignificance of the incident and the importance the clerk ascribes to it, and between the growing irritation of the general, which finally explodes into fury, and the clerk's increasing obsession with the need to obtain forgiveness. Chekhov prevents the reader from feeling any real compassion for Chervyakov by mocking his ludicrous preoccupation. However, the very existence of *chinopochitanie* evokes an uneasy response.

Rank-reverence is presented in another story written that year, "Fat and Thin," the most artistically perfect of his early works. In just a page and a half Chekhov manages to portray a vivid picture of the lives and personalities of two former schoolmates who accidentally meet at a railroad station. Here again the story is built on contrasts. The author includes only those details that reveal the antithetical qualities of the fat man and the thin man. He establishes the difference in their situations with four short sentences:

The fat one had just finished dinner and his buttery lips shone like ripe cherries. He smelled of sherry and fleur d'orange. The thin man had just come out of the train car and was loaded down with suitcases, bundles and cartons. He smelled of ham and coffee grounds. (I, 104).

The thin one is surrounded by all his worldly possessions: his Lutheran wife, his son, and his suitcases and bundles. He summarizes his life in a few sentences and keeps repeating that his wife is a Lutheran, apparently his sole source of distinction. He recalls that he was nicknamed Efhialt when a schoolboy as a result of his being a tattletale. This detail helps to explain his obsequious, dishonest behavior in the second part of the story.

The thin one undergoes a complete change of character as a reaction to the news that his friend is a privy councillor "with two stars." His friendly, cheerful chatter abruptly halts. He presents his family once again, this time not to a friend, but to a high-ranking official.

The opening scene in which the two friends recognize and embrace each other ends with the sentence, "Both were pleasantly stunned" (p. 104), but this time it refers only to the thin man and his family. Their astonishment is not that of joy at seeing an old friend, but rather that of awe in the presence of a superior. In the interim between these two sentences, human feeling has disappeared and been replaced by rank-reverence. The thin one's servility before an old friend is all the more terrible because the situation doesn't warrant it.

As its title suggests, the story "Chameleon" (1884) also describes the automatic transformation that an official undergoes in front of a superior. Khryukin, a jeweler, is bitten by a dog. The police officer Ochumelov, who is passing by, stops to investigate the matter. He is concerned not so much with the man's having been bitten as with the question of to whom the dog belongs. At first he sympathizes with Khryukin, and decides that the dog must be destroyed. Then, when someone suggests that the puppy belongs to General Zhigalov, Ochumelov concludes that she is really too small to bite anyone, that Khryukin must have hurt his hand on a nail and is now trying to blame the poor dog. His attitude again changes as a bystander points out that "the general doesn't have such dogs." "Of course, I know," Ochumelov assures the crowd, and he advises Khryukin to seek compensation (II, 45). When it is finally established that the dog in fact belongs to the general's brother, Ochumelov changes once again, pets the dog, and shouts at Khryukin, "I'll get you yet!"

The mood of the story suggests a kind of existential void. The ominous motif is introduced in the description of the setting: "All is quiet . . . Not a soul on the square . . . the opened doors of stores and taverns look out dejectedly on God's world like hungry jowls" (II, 43). The author never describes Ochumelov's face, but his every action suggests a dull, crude, and mindless force, at once ridiculous and ominous. He is followed by an equally faceless constable, who carries a basket of confiscated gooseberries. Khryukin is presented with no more sympathy. He flatters the policeman and tries to pressure him with, "My brother is also a gendarme" (II, 47). He is half-drunk, disheveled, and his name suggests the grunting of a pig. As it turns out, the puppy bit him because he poked a cigarette into its snout.

The crowd also appears as a mindless mass, changing sides along with the policeman. In the end, after Ochumelov has shouted his threats at the bitten man, " . . . the crowd howls at Khryukin" (II, 45). The only human touch is given by the puppy, who stands at the mercy of these people. "There is an expression of anguish and terror in his moist eyes" (II, 44). To use a term usually applied to Gogol, "Chameleon" is a story of "laughter through tears." Humor fills the dialogue and descriptive passages, but sorrow underlines the text.

In "Melyuzga" (1885) Chekhov probes the consciousness of only one character, yet what emerges in this three-page story is a picture of the abysmal, bureaucratic, half-human world that both produced and destroyed this pitiful clerk. Nevyrazimov is sitting in the office trying to compose an Easter letter to his superior, whom he addresses as "Kindly sir, father, and benefactor" (III, 24). He detests this man "with all his soul" but he is hoping for a raise and knows that he must flatter his superiors on such occasions. Paralleled with Nevyrazimov's miserable life is a lost cockroach that " . . . anxiously runs back and forth" (III, 24) on his desk. The clerk pities him, at the same time pitying himself: "I'll finish my work and will leave, but he will stay here all his cockroach life" (III, 24).

Nevyrazimov dreams of feeling himself a man, but his own definition of the ideal life is limited to "drinking a bit, eat, and fall asleep." He considers three possible ways of escaping his wretched condition: to leave the office, to steal, or to write a denunciation. He despondently rejects each option in turn. Escape promises nothing but the dreariness of his apartment in exchange for the monotony of the office. In order to steal successfully, Nevyrazimov believes one needs an education which he himself lacks. He does not possess the necessary cunning and way with words to write a denunciation, as did his colleague Proshkin, "who reported and went up after that." Nevyrazimov grows increasingly self-pitying and desperate. He looks once more at the unfinished letter he must send to the man he both hates and fears and notices the cockroach again. He squashes the insect with his palm, picks it up, and burns it in his lamp. The last words laconically sum up the theme of "Malyuzga": "And Nevyrazimov felt better" (III, 27).

This final line has many implications. In the time that has elapsed between pitying the cockroach and destroying it, Nevyrazimov has perhaps rid himself of his last trace of human feeling. The relief he feels is a natural reaction to finding a means of self-expression, and of exerting power over a creature that is even less significant than he is.

Once again the theme of the "downtrodden people" is so

presented that the reader feels little sympathy for the clerk. The corruption of the bureaucratic world has penetrated so deeply into the consciousness of all its members that both the oppressors and the oppressed emerge as offensive and disgusting.

The culmination of this theme of servile mentality is presented in Chekhov's famous "Sergeant Prishibeyev." An ex-quartermaster sergeant who had spent years bullying and denouncing whomever he could, Prishibeyev cannot accustom himself to the passive role he must play in the village where he now lives. He intimidates the peasants, spies upon the wives, and breaks up all happy gatherings. He is finally brought to trial for beating up a policeman, the village elder, and a number of others, and is sentenced to one month in jail. All this is incomprehensible to Prishibeyev: "which law says people can be free? . . . I was outraged by the way people nowadays assert their rights and commit acts of insubordination . . . It's under-standable. You have to belt people sometimes" (III, 102).

Some Soviet critics, G. Berdnikov for example, decry Chekhov's failure to "elucidate the political system that created such a hero"[3] and lament the fact that Chekhov was interested in psychology more than in political ideology. While it is true that Chekhov focus-ed on human psychology and never identified himself with a par-ticular ideology, it cannot be said that he ignored the question of Prishibeyev's motivation. Chekhov points out in his understated manner that Sergeant Prishibeyev served in Warsaw in the 1860s dur-ing the Polish rebellion and the ensuing Tsarist terror. The habits that he brought back to his village resulted from his Warsaw train-ing. "For fifteen years we had to endure him," the villagers tell the judge, "Ever since he came back from the army, we have felt like running away from the village. He only torments us" (III, 101). Due to pressure from the censors, Chekhov entitled the story "Klauznik," but when he reworked it for his collected works in 1900, he changed the title to "Sergeant Prishibeyev." He thus plac-ed emphasis on Prishibeyev's army rank as the key to his identity.

Chekhov also modified the story's ending. In the first version the story concludes with a bewildered Prishibeyev crying, "What for? What for?" as he receives his prison sentence. In the final version he leaves the courthouse on his way to the prison, sees a group of peasants wandering around, draws himself up and barks out: "Move along, stop crowding! Go back to your homes!" (III, 104). This change indicates Chekhov's intention once again to prevent the reader from feeling any compassion for a negative character.

Instead of a somewhat pathetic Prishibeyev, victim of an order he cannot understand, we see him in his naked, sadistic offensiveness.

Perhaps the most frightening of all Chekhov's stories is "Zveri" or "The Beasts." At the same time it may be considered to sum up the major themes that have been described here as characterizing his early period. The censors rejected the story, writing to Leikin, "Don't you think that we understand that it isn't about beasts?" The title was then changed to "Cynic," and it was published in *Petersburg Gazette* on December 16, 1885. It is in fact a thinly disguised allegory of life in Russia. The story takes place in a zoo, where the caged animals are at the mercy of a sadistic ex-cadet, a drunkard named Susin. Susin amuses the public by leading it from cage to cage and explaining the particular psychology and tendencies of each animal. He contrasts with delight the free life for which each was destined and their present, total helplessness. He says about the crane, "You are proud, uncompromising, and yet I can take you around the nose in front of the public"; of the monkey, "For a piece of sugar she will bow to her tormentor, not just bow, but will play a jester"; and of a young gazelle, "This one is ready. Just got into the cage and is already dying of tuberculosis. Strange . . . dying and there is still hope in her eyes. That's youth for you" (III, 308 - 309). The audience gradually begins to resent Susin's inhuman treatment of the animals, but this resentment is limited to complaints about the smallness of the cages and the bad food. Susin provokes them to action only when he brings out a rabbit to be eaten by a boa constrictor. Disgusted and nauseated, the people snatch the animal away from its tormentor. Chekhov does not allow kindness to prevail, however: "But a day or two passes and the tranquilized frequenters of the zoo begin to be drawn back to Susin as to vodka or tobacco. They long for his teasing, spine-tingling cynicism" (III, 310).

In "The Beasts" and in most other stories of this period Chekhov concentrates on the cruelty of the tormentor and the complicity of the public. The caged animals, like the puppy in "Chameleon" and the cockroach in "Melyuzga," exist only to serve as the object of this pervasive savagery. It is as if in this early period Chekhov were too angry at the overall stupidity and brutality of life to be concerned with the pain of its victims.

CHAPTER 3

"Images Dear to My Heart"

AFTER the publication of "Requiem" ("Panikhida") on February 15, 1886, the first of Chekhov's stories to appear in the St. Petersburg newspaper *New Times*, he received significant encouragement from a totally unexpected source, Dmitry Grigorovich, a well-known and respected author. Grigorovich wrote (March 25, 1886):

If I speak of your talent, I speak out of conviction. I am almost sixty-five years old, but I still feel so much love for literature, and follow its success with so much ardor and rejoice when I find something living, and gifted, that I cannot refrain—as you see—from holding out both hands to you.[1]

The letter was obviously not so much intended to praise Chekhov's existing work as to implore him not to treat his gift lightly, not to destroy his great promise.

All that is needed is esteem for the talent—which so rarely falls to one's lot. Cease to write hurriedly. I do not know what your financial situation is. If it is poor it would be better for you to go hungry, as we did in our day.[2]

Chekhov was elated and moved by the letter, and his emotional reply to Grigorovich is unique in the collection of his correspondence:

Your letter, my kind and beloved messenger of good news (*blagovestitel'*), struck me like lightning, I almost cried, was overwhelmed by emotion and even now feel that it left a deep trace in my soul . . . I have no strength to judge if I am worthy of this high honor, I only repeat that it astonished me . . . If I have a gift which must be respected, I swear before the purity of your heart that I haven't respected it until now. (March 28, 1886)[3]

Having stated his careless attitude toward his own writing and having explained that it wasn't his hunger that mattered, Chekhov added, "While I wrote I tried as hard as I could not to waste on my stories images that are dear to my heart and which, God knows why, I preserved and kept carefully hidden."

Never again was Chekhov to write such an emotional and naked letter. In fact, on April 4, 1886, he wrote to Bilibin describing Grigorovich's letter in somewhat ironic tones. The irony does not indicate, as one critic suggested, his more natural attitude toward Grigorovich's letter; rather it points again to Chekhov's extreme unwillingness or inability to share something intimate with anyone else.

The year 1886 was a significant one in that Chekhov's comic and satirical sketches were gradually replaced by stories dealing with human emotions and sorrow. The competence with which Chekhov handled such stories as "Toska" or "Vanka" perhaps explains how, though his work centered on satire, the images dear to his heart were hidden and preserved by him.

Later Chekhov became known as the creator of what is called in Russian criticism "the literature of mood" (*literatura nastroenija*), where not action but the evocation of a special, elusive, and undefined mood is the distinctive characteristic of a story. "Toska," first published on January 27, 1886, in *Petersburgskaya gazeta*, and still considered as one of his masterpieces, is a perfect example of that kind of moody story.

The narrative follows the coachman Iona Potapov as he drives his fares around St. Petersburg; Iona's son has just died and the coachman tries to lessen his grief by sharing it with his customers. Occupied with their own shallow affairs, they only shout at him to drive faster. When Iona tries to tell his sad story to a fellow coachman, his colleague falls asleep. Finally, ignored by everyone else, Iona begins to talk to the only creature that will listen to him: his horse.

The point of the story is to create in the reader the same feeling of *toska* (sorrowful longing) that drives Iona from the unresponsive human beings to his horse. The work is carefully designed to attain that end. As A. N. Vasil'eva displays in her superb stylistic analysis of the story,[4] the first paragraph forecasts the direction the tale will take. Within these nine perfectly balanced sentences, Chekhov gradually creates a mood of death-like immobility, monotony, and despair which imagistically unites Iona with his mare.

The paragraph opens with a two-word sentence in the nominative case: "Evening twilight" (IV, 17), which introduces the lack of action in the following sentences. It suggests an atmosphere of nebulous colors and muted sounds. By describing the snow as "lazily circling" and "settling in thin, soft layers" (IV, 17), Chekhov emphasizes the static mood of the scene. The three sentences describing Iona and the three sentences which describe his horse further develop the impression of immobility. Iona is "white as a ghost," a "human body . . . sitting very still on his box." The mare "too, was white, and quite motionless" (IV, 17). Chekhov used the short adjective *bel* rather than the long form *belyi*. In Russian, as Vasil'eva notes, this makes "white" not a quality, but a state of being.[5]

The three sentences devoted exclusively to the horse exhibit an interesting tonal development. Chekhov first refers to the animal as *loshadenka*, a rather contemptuous label. He then switches to the affectionate *loshadka*, and finally brings the reader even closer to her by stating that "she is plunged in deep thought" (IV, 17). The author continues this humanizing of the mare in the last sentence of the first paragraph, as he unites her with the man in summing up their common past and future: "He, who was torn from the plow, from the familiar, gray surroundings, and thrown into a slough full of monstrous lights, ceaseless cacophony and people running, he cannot but think . . ." (IV, 17).

The rest of "Toska" is a dramatization of this last sentence. The grief-filled immobility of Iona and the horse is shattered by the rude human voices of people who are too impatient to listen to Iona's story. Even though Chekhov provides a vivid picture of human callousness through both dialogue and action, the constant sorrow that Iona feels is even more pervasive. Relief comes only at the end of the story in the one moment of tenderness when Iona addresses his horse as "brother mare" and, "surrendering to his grief" (IV, 21), begins to tell her of his son.

Chekhov centered his attention once again on the portrayal of a state of human misery in "Vanka" (1886). Although written from an omniscient point of view, the narrative focus is on a young boy's consciousness as revealed in a letter he is writing to his grandfather, and the reveries that accompany it. He has been sent to Moscow as a shoemaker's apprentice, and he begs his grandfather to bring him home to the village. The reader feels the despair of this nine-year-old boy through the contrast between his wretched existence in the city and his tender memories of life in the village.

Chekhov begins to create an ominous impression of life in the city in the first paragraph. The opening lines are filled with images of darkness. As he pauses from his writing, afraid that his master will return home unexpectedly and beat him, Vanka's gaze falls upon "the dark ikon," and he peers anxiously into the "dark window." By contrast, when "dark" appears in connection with Vanka's memories of the village, it expresses joy and beauty, not fear: "The night was dark, but the whole white-roofed village with its snowdrifts and trees silvered with hoarfrost and smoke streaming from the chimneys could be seen clearly. The heavens were sprinkled with gay, glittering stars, and the Milky Way stood out as clearly as if it had been washed and scrubbed with snow for the holidays" (IV, 311).

Vanka's memories are not idealized or made sentimental. His grandfather is no saint. A sixty-five-year-old drunkard who passes his time joking with the cooks and pinching maids, he amuses himself by giving snuff to the dogs. Even the dog Eel (Vyun) conceals "a most Jesuitical malice" (IV, 310) beneath his obsequiousness and humility. Vanka knows all this, and yet he still wants to return. It is because this miserable life appears so desirable to him that his present anguish is revealed so vividly. He writes his grandfather, "I'll grind snuff for you, I will pray to God for you, and if I ever do anything wrong, you can flog me all you like . . . If you'll do this for me, I'll feed you when I grow up, and won't let anyone harm you, and when you die, I'll pray for the repose of your soul . . ." (IV, 311). An intelligent and perceptive child, Vanka has recognized the need for submission, yet he still dreams.

The story's pathetic atmosphere is reinforced by an ironic twist at the end: Vanka naively addresses the letter "To grandfather in the village" (IV, 312) and drops it in a mailbox. He returns to the household he hates and falls asleep dreaming of his grandfather receiving the letter and reading it to the cooks. This zero ending allows the pathos to remain undisturbed; it leaves the reader's imagination to complete the story.

Chekhov included "Vanka" in a collection of stories about children entitled *Detvora* (Children), published in 1889. He excluded a story very similar to "Vanka," "Sleepy" (Spat' khochetsia, 1888) which Tolstoi considered one of Chekhov's very best tales. It too depicts a child, Varka, who is totally at the mercy of cruel adults. However, unlike Vanka, Varka is deprived of any illusory hope. In the letter to his grandfather Vanka writes that his master

had given him a beating the day before, "because when I was rocking the baby in the cradle, I unfortunately fell asleep . . . They
make me sleep in the passageway, and when the baby cries, I don't
get any sleep at all because I have to rock the cradle" (IV, 311). In
"Sleepy" Chekhov isolates this experience and probes Varka's consciousness as she is driven insane by a lack of rest.

As in "Toska" Chekhov sets the tone that will govern the rest of
the story in the first paragraph. The first sentence consists of one
word: "Night" (VI, 127). Varka, a thirteen-year-old servant girl, is
rocking the baby, trying to stay awake. With a few descriptive
details Chekhov creates a mood of menacing constriction: "Across
the entire room, from corner to corner, stretched a rope with diapers
and an enormous pair of black trousers hanging down from it. A
great patch of green light reflects upward from the image-lamp on
the ceiling, and diapers and trousers cast long shadows onto the
stove, onto the cradle, and onto Varka . . . When the lamplight
begins to flicker, the patch and the shadows come alive and are set
in motion as though by a wind. It is stuffy . . ." (VI, 127).

The reader sees and feels these objects through Varka's exhausted
senses. As she grows more and more tired they become sinister symbols of the situation that compels the girl to stay awake. Opposed to
these are sounds such as crickets singing in the stove, the cradle's
creaking, and the snoring of the master and mistress, sounds which
lure Varka to forbidden sleep. At this point in the story these two
forces are separated and represent adversaries, but at the end they
will merge into a single tyranny taking possession of Varka's mind.
The green patch and the shadows are a recurring leitmotif announcing the girl's hallucinations, then her madness, and finally the
death of the baby, whom Varka kills in order to escape into that
other world of cricket cries and blissful sleep.

This sensual impressionism allows Chekhov to avoid narrative intrusion, which would destroy the mood of "sleep-yearning." The
reader learns of Varka's past through the completely assimilated
flashbacks of her reveries and dreams. This device must also be
viewed as a function of Chekhov's desire to depict a person drifting
in and out of sleep and dreams. The shadows and green patch
". . . climb into her half-open, motionless eyes" (VI, 128) and are
transformed by her exhausted mind into images of people falling
into mud and thus into sleep. These confused pictures finally take
the form of half-memories and half-visions, as Varka dreams of her
father's death. They also serve to introduce explicitly the theme of
death:

Varka slipped away into the forest and gave herself up to weeping, and suddenly someone hit her across the nape of the neck with such force that she cracked her forehead against a birch tree. Then she looked up and saw it was her master, the shoemaker. (VI, 129)

Chekhov thus captures the hazy interdependence and alternation between the conscious world and the dream world.

Varka cannot obey her master, however, because the green patch and shadows "once again possess her brain" (VI, 129). She begins another dream, this one of her mother begging for alms, but her mother's pleading, "Give something for the love of Christ" (VI, 129) is suddenly replaced by her mistress's harsh "Give me the baby!" (VI, 129). With the approach of morning, the shadows and green patch wane and lose their power over the girl. It is easier to stay awake in the daylight, and she is kept busy obeying orders to wash the staircase, clean the booths, run to the store for vodka, and light the samovar. Although her masters deprive her not only of sleep, but even of rest, she at least can look forward to the night, when she will sleep. In her numb dismay, however, she learns that she must repeat the ordeal of the night before. The same patch, the shadows, the cricket cries, again oppress her tired brain. Varka stares incomprehensibly at the green patch, trying to understand just who her enemy is. The baby cries, and Varka suddenly realizes the cause of her misery.

Her enemy was the baby. She laughed aloud. She was astonished how simple it all was! It seemed to her that the shadows, the cricket, the green stain—all of them were smiling in astonishment. (VI, 131)

The circle has thus been closed. Unable to understand the forces that are destroying her life, Varka kills another child as ignorant and innocent as herself. In the closing sentence Chekhov emphasizes the irony and horror of the situation, indicating Varka's fate with the final words: "Having strangled the child, she quickly lies down on the floor, laughing with joy that she can finally sleep, and in a minute she is already asleep as though she were dead" (VI, 131). The word "Night" which opened this story is now moved onto a symbolic plane.

I   "The Steppe" *1888*

In the year 1888, Chekhov finally heeded Grigorovich's admonition to reduce the number of his short stories to ten a year, and began a much longer work, "The Steppe." With characteristic self-irony Chekhov wrote to I.L. Shcheglov:

Began a little trifle for the *Northern Herald* (that literary "widows' house"). I don't know when I'll finish it. The thought that I am writing for a "fat journal" and that people will view my trifle more seriously than is necessary pushes my elbow as the devil pushes a monk. I am writing a steppe story. I am writing it but I don't feel that it smells of hay. (January 1, 1888)[6]

But the evidence that Chekhov hardly considered "The Steppe" a trifle can be found in a letter to Lazarev-Gruzinsky written on February 4, 1888:

I spent a lot of juice, energy and phosphor on my "Steppe." I wrote with tension, strained myself, squeezed it out of myself and am disgustingly exhausted. I don't know if I succeeded or not with it, but in any case it is my chef d'oeuvre, I can't do any better than that, and so your comforting that "things at times don't turn out (in case of unsuccess)[7] can't comfort me."

The fact that Chekhov was writing his first long story for the *Northern Herald,* one of the so-called "fat journals" that maintained the highest literary standards of the time, might have pushed his elbow, but vanity was not the moving force behind the writing of this story.

When, in 1887, Chekhov journeyed to the Don Steppe it was in hopes to "greet the spring and refresh my memory on things that have already begun to grow dim" (Letter to A.S. Souvorin, Feb. 10, 1887).[8] It was in that region, so Russian in its landscape, so different from the cities where Chekhov lived since he left Taganrog, that he hoped to reawake his creative energies. The journey, though it was not apparent to him immediately, did indeed refresh his memory and reopen some dormant sources, for the subtly violent landscape became not only the setting for several of his stories ("The Steppe," "The Beauties," "Happiness and Lights") but led Chekhov back to his desire to write a novel.

In my "Steppe", through all the eight chapters, I take a nine-year-old boy who, having gone to Petersburg or to Moscow, will inevitably end up badly. If the "Steppe" would have even a little success, then I would continue with it. I wrote it on purpose in a way so that it would give the impression of an unfinished work. (letter to D.V. Grigorovich, Feb. 5, 1888).[9]

"The Steppe" was greeted with mixed reactions from the critics. Pleshcheev, one of the editors of the *Northern Herald,* praised it highly, but others, like P.N. Ostrovsky, a brother of the famous playwright, wrote in a letter that the story, ". . . has no inner organization . . . has no center . . . and at times it is the child, at times it is the steppe that draws the attention of the reader" (A.P. Čechov i nas kraj, Rostov na Donu 1935, p. 136).[10]

The story concerns three travelers who set out early in the morning across the steppe: a merchant, Ivan Ivanitch Kuzmichov, his 9-year-old nephew, Egorushka, and a priest, Father Khristofor. The two men are on their way to sell wool; the boy is on his way to school. They are in search of Varlamov whose business acumen is legendary and to whom they intend to sell their wool. In the evening they come to a posting house which is run by a Jew Moisei Moiseitch and his family, including his embittered brother Solomon. Solomon burnt his inheritance in the stove because he feels himself above the sordid acquisitiveness but harbors a self-destructive malevolence. Before the three travelers leave Countess Dranitskaya appears, also in search of Varlamov. Egorushka is impressed by her beauty, likening her to a solitary poplar tree they passed that day on the steppe. Later that evening Egorushka is left in the wagoners' care.

As the journey progresses, Egorushka becomes acquainted with the wagoners and their particular tale of woe. After a violent storm Egorushka becomes ill. When he meets again with his uncle, who had successfully completed his business, Egorushka recovers quickly and is taken to the home of an old friend of his mother where he will live while attending school.

Although "The Steppe" has no central social message, it is united artistically by its theme and imagery. The journey of the young boy Egorushka assumes an epic quality where the basic confrontation between quixotic imagination and the bare brutality of life creates an impressionistic image of reality.

Viktor Shklovsky has noted in his book *Zametki o proze russkikh klassikov* (Notes about the prose of Russian Classics)[11] that the opening lines of "The Steppe" immediately establish a comparative association with Gogol's *Dead Souls:*

> . . . Into the gates of the inn of the provincial town of NN there drove a rather pretty little chaise on springs, of the type customarily used by bachelors, such as retired lieutenant colonels, staff captains, landowners

with about one-hundred serfs—in short by all those who are called "gentlemen of a middling sort." *(Dead Souls)*

Early one morning in July a shabby covered chaise, one of those antediluvian chaises without springs in which no one travels in Russia nowadays, except merchants, clerks, dealers, and the less well-to-do among priests, drove out of N., the principal town of the province of Z, and rumbled along the posting-track. ("The Steppe," VI, 132)

Other themes and techniques used by Chekhov in "The Steppe" are also reminiscent of *Dead Souls*. Both works contrast the beauty and splendor of nature with the mediocrity of bourgeois pursuits. Like Chichikov, Egorushka's uncle Kuzmichov and the priest Khristofor, are chiefly concerned with mercantile profit, the enjoyment of meals, and voicing their stale beliefs. Chekhov's stylistic techniques also mimic several of Gogol's devices in *Dead Souls*. In both works nature is often personified and characters are drawn by the repetition of certain epithets, by hyperbole, by their resemblance to animals, and by their particular speech mannerisms. The similarities in characterization become especially evident from a comparison between Gogol's Manilov and Chekhov's innkeeper Moisei Moiseich (*Dead Souls*, pp. 21 - 41; "The Steppe," VI, 146 - 156).[12]

Stylistically, "The Steppe" is perhaps one of Chekhov's most tightly woven, perfect works. The first chapter introduces the central images that will reappear throughout the narrative in accordance with Egorushka's psychological state, and will develop the theme of the story. Egorushka's naiveté and his romantic illusions are first indicated by his clothing: he wears a red shirt that billows "like a balloon on his back" and "a new hat with a peacock's feather" (VI, 133). His imaginative perception of a windmill and his identification of it as a "sorcerer" (VI, 138) further reveal Egorushka's fanciful nature.

Juxtaposed to the quixotic windmill whose wings suggest an imaginary representation of reality are the wings of a hawk "that suddenly halted in the air as though pondering the dreariness of life, then fluttered its wings and flew like an arrow over the steppe" (VI, 135). This dreariness is echoed by the "disillusioned steppe" suffering from the July heat, where "everything living was hushed" (VI, 135). The cruel indifference of life is finally unmistakably signified by the wild steppe dogs that "surrounded the chaise, with their shaggy spider-like muzzles and their eyes red with anger" and that "seemed ready to tear them to pieces." These dogs belong to Varlamov, the wealthy merchant to whom Kusmichov and Khristofor will sell their wool and whose identity is linked with the triumph of cunning on the steppe (see VI, 188 - 190).

In the second chapter the carriage halts by a stream, during which time Egorushka becomes increasingly conscious of the "dreariness" of the steppe first signified in the image of a hawk. This motif is now developed with the "subdued dreary melancholy" (VI, 142) of a peasant woman's song, which gives the impression that

the grass itself was singing, in its song, withered and half-dead, it was without words, but plaintively and passionately, urging that it was not to blame that the sun was burning it for no fault of its own; it urged that it ardently longed to live, that it was young and might have been beautiful but for the heat and the drought . . . . (VI, 142)

This dreary song is reinforced by the heavy, oppressive air, and by the repeated image of the ominous hawk from chapter one. However, the distant although audible thunder at the end of chapter two offers a hope of redemptive rain. Nature has the power to renew life as well as to destroy it, but again "the invisible oppressive force gradually riveted its fetters on the wind and air, laid the dust, and the stillness came back. The cloud hid, the sun-baked hills frowned submissively, the air grew calm, and only somewhere the troubled lapwings wailed and lamented their destiny" (VI, 146).

In the evening the three travelers arrive at Moisei Moiseitch's inn, where Egorushka meets a colorful assortment of people. Opposed to the effusive, saccharinely sweet innkeeper and his wife is Solomon: a "short young Jew with a beak-like nose, with a bald patch surrounded by rough, curly hair. . . He was dressed in a short and very shabby reefer jacket, with rounded lappets and short sleeves, . . . so that he looked skimpy and short-tailed like an unfledged bird . . . (VI, 146, 149). Solomon's bird-like physiognomy and his contemptuous, "gleaming sarcastic eyes" (VI, 149) identify him with the destructive dreariness of the steppe hawk. He is totally estranged from the merchants' life and values, but although Solomon has renounced material gain to "become more like a man" than Varlamov, there is something evil and primitive in his mocking cynicism (VI, 155).

However, the brief entrance of the beautiful Countess Dranitskaya at the end of this chapter introduces a lyrical tone into the narrative. Her description is reminiscent of the beautiful women in Gogol's fairy tales, and she inspires the same associations in Egorushka:

All at once, quite unexpectedly, Egorushka saw half an inch from his eyes velvety black eyebrows, big brown eyes, delicate feminine cheeks with dimples, from which smiles seemed radiating all over the face like sunbeams. There was a glorious scent . . . . "How beautiful she is," thought Egorushka . . . His drowsy brain uterly refused ordinary thoughts, was in a cloud and retained only fantastic fairy-tale images, which have the advantage of springing into the brain of themselves without any effort on the part of thinker. (VI, 157)

The steppe has also become fantastically beautiful in the cool, cleansing evening darkness. Chekhov's impressionistic description of its charms is among the most poetic he has written:

There is a scent of hay and dry grass and belated flowers, but the scent is heavy, sweetly mawkish and soft. . . And when the moon rises the night becomes pale and dim. The mist seems to have passed away. The air is transparent, fresh and warm; one can see well in all directions and even distinguish the separate stalks of grass by the wayside. Stones and bits of pots can be seen at a long distance. Broad shadows move across the plain-like clouds in the sky, and in the inconceivable distance, . . . misty monstrous shapes rise up and huddle one against another . . . It is rather uncanny . . . Of the unfathomable depth and infinity of the sky one can only form a conception at sea and on the steppe by night when the moon is shining. It looks down languid and alluring, and its caressing sweetness makes one giddy. (VI, 160)

A new phase of the story begins when Egorushka is transferred to the care of Varlamov's wagon drivers, who are intimately linked with life on the steppe. Likewise, the landscape has changed: "There were no hills now, but on all sides, wherever one looked, there stretched the brown cheerless plain . . ." (VI, 162). Egorushka fantasizes about the folk heroes who once strode across this great expanse of land, which is deromanticized by Chekhov's observation that "Hawks, falcons and crows sat on wires and looked indifferently at the moving wagons" (VI, 162).

The quality that all Varmolov's peasant workers share is their suffering. The old man Pantelei has almost frozen to death more than once, Vasya has had part of his jaw destroyed in a sulfur-factory, Emelyan has lost his fine singing voice, and even the sadistic Dymov suffers from "the dreariness of life."

The physical description of Emelyan and his lyrical nature immediately associate him with the symbol of the windmills in chapter one, "which in the distance looked like tiny men waving their arms." Emelyan also waves his arms imitating a concert conductor, and he is constantly engaged in a doomed battle to regain his singing voice. Emelyan is thus linked to the themes of the indifference of nature and unfledged dreams: he is inspired by life at the same time that he is repressed by it:

. . . Emelyan sang alone. He waved both arms, nodded his head, opened his mouth, but nothing came from his throat but a discordant gasp. He sang with his arms, with his head, with his eyes, even with swelling on his face; he sang passionately with anguish, and the more he strained his chest to extract at least one note from it, the more discordant were his gasps . . . . (VI, 187)

Contrasted to Emelyan is the brutal Dymov, who is a destructive agent of death. He first kills a harmless grass snake and later is intent upon pushing Egorushka, who fears to be drowned, under water.

Egorushka is sensitive to the suffering of those around him, and again his consciousness is brought to the theme of death and despair:

When you gaze a long while fixedly at the deep sky, thoughts and feelings for some reason merge in a sense of loneliness. One begins to feel hopelessly solitary, and everything one used to look upon as near and akin becomes infinitely remote and valueless . . . One is reminded of the solitude awaiting each one of us in the grave, and the reality of life seems awful . . . full of despair . . . . (VI, 177)

This theme is later applied to Russia itself, where "life is terrible and marvelous, and so, however terrible a story you tell in Russia, . . . it always finds an echo of reality in the listener" (VI, 183).

The storm at the end of chapter seven inspires this sort of terror in Egorushka, who in order to explain its deafening din believes that folklore giants are once again striding across the plain:

"Grandfather, the giants!" Egorushka shouted to him in tears. He was convinced that the thunder would kill him in another minute, that he would accidentally open his eyes and see the terrible giants, and he left off crossing himself, calling the old man and thinking of his mother . . . . (VI, 195 - 96)

In the last chapter of "The Steppe" Egorushka is reunited with his uncle and the priest, by which time he has already been taken ill from exposure to the storm. He recovers quickly and is entrusted to the care of his mother's friend Nastasya Petrovna Toskunova. The story ends inconclusively with Egorushka's searching question: "What will life be like?" The steppe has been crossed, and Egorushka has been initiated into many of life's mysteries and horrors. However, the impression is created that he has yet to face greater trials before he will reach the answer to that question.

II "Lights" 1888

Following "The Steppe," Chekhov began to work on a story with a philosophical theme, "Lights." As is apparent from his correspondence of that period (February 1888 to May 1888) the writing of this philosophical work was quite difficult for Chekhov. The theme he had chosen, that of nihilism, was topical at the time in Russia, but Chekhov with his distaste for offering solutions was interested in stating the problem correctly rather than with leading his narration to some moral conclusion which, he knew, the editors expected of him. Indeed, when the story was finished Suvorin complained to its author that he did nothing to solve the question of pessimism. To that Chekhov replied:

It seems to me that it is not fiction writers who ought to decide such questions as pessimism, God, etc. The fiction writers' function is purely to describe who talked or thought about God or pessimism, how and under what circumstances. The artist must be, not the judge of his characters and of what they say, but merely a dispassionate observer. (May 30, 1888)[13]

"Lights" portrays two antithetical characters, the engineer Ananev and his assistant young Baron von Shtenberg. It begins as Ananev comforts a nervous dog named Azorka, thus revealing his compassionate nature. Ananev is joined by von Shtenberg and the narrator, a doctor spending the night with them. The three men silently contemplate the night-time visits of a lonely steppe, empty save for a few lights stretching out to the horizon. This scene embodies the mood of the story, as it provokes the narrator to ponder the mystery of the universe:

The lights were motionless. There seemed to be something in common between them and the stillness of the night and the disconsolate song of the telegraph wire. It seemed as though some weighty secret were busied under the embankment and only the lights, the night, and the wires knew of it. (VI, 359)

Ananev sees the lights as a testament to man's ability to tame the elements and to improve his lot in the world. Von Shtenberg, on the other hand, experiences a sentiment closer to that of the narrator. The lights remind him of the lights that must have burned in the towns of long-departed civilizations and cause him to reflect on the transitoriness of all human endeavor.

These contrasting reactions embody the differences between the two men. Ananev is in the "prime of life," neither too old nor too young. He is content and satisfied with life, and loves his family dearly. He is thus a good foil for the young student von Shtenberg, who does everything with the same degree of indifference. He feels that life is a mockery of man in that everyone must inevitably die, and thus concludes that all dreams and struggles are in vain. Von Shtenberg's resigned torpor is the opposite of Ananev's contentment, which is achieved by living. The student has become indifferent as a result of reasoning and deducing that life is meaningless. To Ananev these "Solomon thoughts" (VI, 360) are fit for the end of life, not for its beginning. Once a man reaches this conclusion he is unable to do anything, and is ready for death:

Thoughts of the aimlessness of life, of the insignificance and transitoriness of the visible world, Solomon's "vanity of vanities" have been, and are to this day, the highest and final stage in the realm of thought. The thinker reaches that stage and comes to a halt! There is nowhere further to go. The activity of the normal brain is completed with this, and that is natural and in the order of things. Our misfortune is that we begin thinking at that end. What normal people end with we begin with. From the first start, as soon as the brain begins working independently, we mount to the very topmost, final step and refuse to know anything about the steps below. (VI, 363)

The older man feels that such premature skepticism sours the life of him who experiences it. Even worse, such an attitude inevitably affects the life of others:

Besides being corrupted ourselves, we bring poison into the lives of those surrounding us. It would be all right if, with our pessimism, we renounced life and went to live in a cave, or made haste to die, but, as it is, in obedience to the universal law, we live, feel, love women, bring up children, construct railways! (VI, 364)

The engineer declares that he speaks with authority: he was once very much like the young baron, and his indifference nearly ruined the life of a trusting soul. The bulk of the story consists of Ananev's subsequent narration.

When he was young, Ananev explains, his emotions were buried beneath a morass of rationality. His indifference compelled him to view ironically any spontaneous feeling he might have, and his disregard of any responsibility ("What matters, if we will all soon be dead?" [VI, 367]) made him a cold man. With this coldness and cynicism he approached Kisochka, a childhood friend he encounters during a short trip to his native town. She is a sensitive, miserable woman, trapped in a stagnant life and hungry for love and affection, in short, ready material for a seduction: "My sense guessed and my conscience whispered to me, happy and indifferent, that in front of me stands a good, well-meaning, loving, but tormented person" (VI, 374). He seduces her, reasoning that such actions could not be considered reprehensible in this meaningless world. Then he subsequently abandons her. However, he felt incessant guilt and a vague anxiety which he at last identified as the rebuke of his conscience: "I had committed a crime which is equal to murder" (VI, 383). Young Ananev finally did repent, and in so doing sowed the seeds of his future humanism.

Notwithstanding the fact that Ananev's story comprises at least two-thirds of the work, Chekhov does not weigh the scales in favor of such moral redemption. In the beginning of the "Lights" Ananev comforts a dog while von Shtenberg calls him a good man for it. However, in point of fact these two men do not act very differently. An incident is presented at the end of the story that appears to be a routine day for the student and the engineer, and thus can be used to judge them:

Ananev and the student, both in their underclothes and barefooted, were angrily and impatiently explaining to a peasant who was standing before them bare-headed, with his whip in his hand, apparently not understanding them. Both faces looked preoccupied with workday cares. (VI, 387)

The student, a pessimist who hasn't lived to test his theory, and the humanist, supposedly wise after the experience of life, act in exactly the same way in their daily life. The narrator notices this, and the answers to the question of life's meaning which Ananev had given him dissipate like the morning fog. As he drives away, the narrator's perception of the landscape harmonizes with his thought into a pessimistic image of incomprehensibility:

And when I lashed my horse and galloped along the line, and when a little
later I saw nothing before me but the endless gloomy plain and the cold
overcast sky, I recalled the questions which were discussed in the night. I
pondered while the sun-scorched plain, the immense sky, the oak forest,
dark on the horizon and the hazy distance, seemed to say to me:
"Yes, there's no understanding anything in this world!" The sun began to
rise . . . . (VI, 388)

Some critics have found this indefinite ending puzzling. I.L.
Leontiev-Shcheglov, a young writer, told Chekhov that the conclusion unfortunately lacked a statement. The author was well aware of
this, and even were it stylistically possible for him to intrude into
the story, Chekhov did not consider himself capable of answering
the question of life's meaning:

A psychologist should not pretend to understand what he does not understand. Moreover, a psychologist should not convey the impression that he
understands what no one understands. We shall not play the charlatan, and
we will declare frankly that nothing is clear in this world. Only fools and
charlatans know and understand everything. (To Shcheglov, June 9, 1888)[14]

Despite the longing for a definite moral attitude, Chekhov would
not accept an abstract dictum which his own experience refuted.
The search for a reconciliation between skepticism and humanism
would continue into his later, more ambitious works.

CHAPTER 4

Search for a Philosophy of Life

THE seeming control and calm with which Chekhov described
the dreary scenes of life earned him a reputation of passive
gentleness and humility, or else accusations of being politically and
sociologically indifferent. It was true that of all the Russian writers
Chekhov never tried to enthrone his personal opinions into prin-
ciples. Preaching and moralizing were repugnant to him, and he
later said that in order to describe the trees in the garden one
doesn't have to label them. But labeling was exactly what the critics
expected from a Russian writer, whose role they perceived as a
light-carrier, not as one who describes without prescribing. Furthermore, they expected a writer to have firm political convictions, to
advance reforms, and to register protest.

And although Chekhov never expressed any tendency to be a
reformer and was quite satisfied to remain an observer of human
life, he did not take himself so lightly as a man or a writer to remain
indifferent to unjust accusation. Thus when V. M. Lavrov, one of
the editors of the *Russian Thought* magazine, attacked him in his
article (March, 1890) as a "priest of unprincipled writing,"
Chekhov, a most private man who guarded his inner world even
from his most intimate friends, wrote to Lavrov (April 10, 1890)

I have never been an unprincipled writer or a scoundrel which is the same
thing. It is true that my literary activities were composed of many unending
mistakes, at times crude ones, but this is explainable in terms of my ability
and not whether I am a good or a bad man. In short I have many stories
and articles that I would gladly throw out for their usefulness, but I don't
have a single line for which I could feel ashamed.[1]

This letter together with such probing stories as "Gusev," "A
Boring Story," and "The Duel," must have served to modify
Lavrov's opinion of Chekhov. Two years later he sent a note of

56

apology to him, asking Chekhov to forget the entire incident and suggesting that he start to contribute material to *Russian Thought*. From that point on Chekhov maintained a close relationship with the magazine and its liberal point of view, and published his story, "Ward Number Six," in that journal.

But if the chiding of the critics and fellow writers did not persuade him of the necessity to be a moral arbitrator, the writings of Lev Tolstoi nevertheless held him in their spell. Of the great moralizer he said, in a letter to Suvorin, that Tolstoi's philosophy "deeply affected me and possessed me for about six or seven years."

Chekhov, having come from the peasant class, did not share Tolstoi's predilection for peasant blouses and for mowing the fields. He said he liked soft carpets, comfort, and beautiful women, and nowhere in his writing or in his private correspondence is there any association between sex and sin as it is encountered in Tolstoi. Nor did he share Tolstoi's interest in religious faith. But Chekhov, a most gentle man, though he knew very well the potentiality of evil and cruelty in all human beings, abhorred violence. Tolstoi's doctrine of nonresistance to evil must have appealed to him. This theme appears in several of Chekhov's stories such as *Good People* (1886) and *The Meeting* (1887).

In *Good People* the question of nonresistance to evil is directly explored as it is perceived by two different consciousnesses: a columnist who writes on intellectual matters and his physician sister who wants to devote her life to doctoring the peasants. In *The Meeting*, the moralizing is even more explicit; it is a tale about a thief who steals from a peasant the money that he collected for rebuilding the church and who gradually repents under the influence of the peasant's refusal to resist his crime in any way. Both stories are written in a tone that is unusual for Chekhov, the tone in which the didactic folk-tales were written in Russian literature, with the kind of melancholy calmness that laments the state of human affairs.

It is apparent from these stories that Chekhov at that time was trying to resolve within himself the problem of choice between solidarity and solitude, whether or not he should devote himself to social issues and healing or to dedicate his full energies to writing. And even if his whole being was on the side of his craft, he must have had doubts as to its particular value. The fact that a great writer, like Lev Tolstoi, was preaching the supremacy of morality over art must have accentuated his own doubts. Perhaps his desire to go to the penal colony on Sakhalin Island was a way of resolving this dilemma. Perhaps, too, he understood after his return that a writer in his solitude need not give up solidarity with the insulted and the injured, for his short story, "Gusev," conveys much more powerfully the plight of the oppressed and.passive people than his long and scholarly work, *Sakhalin Island.*

This struggle within himself and the struggle to overcome Tolstoi's influence are best reflected in his fictional writing. It was on September 8, 1891, that he wrote Suvorin on reading "The Kreutzer Sonata," "The devil take the philosophy of the great ones of this world. All the great sages are as despotic as generals, and as ignorant and as indelicate as generals, because they feel secure. Diogenes spat in people's faces, knowing that he would not suffer for it. Tolstoi abuses doctors as scoundrels, and displays his ignorance in great questions because he is just such a Diogenes who won't be locked up, or abused in newspapers."[2]

Chekhov had already challenged Tolstoi in "The Boring Story," and in August, 1891, he was working on another story, "The Duel," which, as he wrote Suvorin (August 6, 1891), exhausted him and cost him one pound of nerves. "The Duel" takes up Tolstoi's gospel of moral redemption through Christian virtues and puts it in a more mundane but human perspective. It was in the spring of 1892 that Chekhov finally took on Tolstoi's doctrine of nonresistance to evil in his "Ward Number Six." He continued his polemic with Tolstoi in stories like "My Life," and, perhaps in response to his own questions about people of exceptional intelligence and imagination, he wrote "The Black Monk," which portrays a man who deludes himself in thinking that he is the bearer of truth. Chekhov continued to polemicize with Tolstoi to the end of his life, but the struggle to overcome the other writer's influence and thus to arrive at some sort of philosophy of his own is best revealed in the following stories.

I "A Boring Story" *1889*

"A Boring Story" undertakes a full-scale probe of one man's existence, not simply showing it in a sketch, but examining closely the forces that have led this man to an existential void, and in so doing, depicting the horror of a life without meaning. At the same time it exhibits perfectly Chekhov's ability to shape the reader's response without having to resort to direct statement.

Chekhov first conceived the story at the end of 1888. In discussing it with Suvorin (November 28, 1888) he writes that the story would end with "something that was known long ago: that a conscious life without a definite world view is not life, but a burden, a horror."[3] The hero would be young, impetuous, healthy, a lover of women, nature, and philosophy. This conception apparently did not satisfy him, and he left the story in order to work on his play *Ivanov*. He picked it up again during the summer of 1889. References to it begin to appear in letters to Pleshcheyev which testify to his growing absorption with the story: "I've never written anything like it; the motifs are completely new to me" (September 3, 1889[4]).

When "A Boring Story" was published in *Northern Bulletin* in November of 1889, critics compared it unfavorably with Tolstoi's "Death of Ivan Ilich." There are similarities between Ivan Ilich and the protagonist of Chekhov's story, Professor Nikolai Stepanovich: both are reexamining their lives in the face of imminent death, both conclude that their lives have lacked something genuine and vital, and both are estranged from their respective families. It is possible that Chekhov was indeed influenced by Tolstoi when he wrote "A Boring Story," but this does not at all detract from the story's importance. If he did borrow Tolstoi's main theme, Chekhov deepened it and gave it a more tragic aspect. Unlike Tolstoi, he could not find a simple solution for his hero. Nikolai Stepanovich does not "see the light" in the end, nor was he "in the dark" from the beginning. Rather he is staring into a void throughout the story.

Chekhov transformed the young and impetuous hero of his original version into a sixty-two-year-old professor. Nikolai Stepanovich is a fully conscious man who has led a rational life devoted to science and the teaching of medicine. Whereas Ivan Ilich's existence centered mainly around the shallow pursuit of personal advancement, the work of Chekhov's professor brought him fulfillment in that it contributed, at least indirectly, to the betterment of mankind. Nikolai Stepanovich does not question the value of his profession when he reexamines his life, but he does realize that it has left him estranged from the people closest to him. The usefulness of his work is contrasted with the barrenness of his personal relationships, so that a split emerges between his professional and his private self.

This schism is immediately evident in the first three paragraphs, as Chekhov separates the professor-narrator from his public image. The narrative, in the form of a confessional monologue, begins with a seemingly omniscient point of view: "There lives in Russia a certain Honored Professor Nikolai Stepanovich . . ." (VII, 15). The narrator proceeds to enumerate dispassionately those qualities that characterize this Nikolai Stepanovich before he finally informs the reader that he and the professor are one and the same person: "All of this, and a great deal more that might be said, constitutes what is called my 'name.' " (VII, 15). The repetition of the word "name" eight times in these paragraphs serves to underline Nikolai Stepanovich's objectivization of his identity and his conviction that "My name is as brilliant and attractive as I myself am dull and unprepossessing" (VII, 16). The professor is even unable to fathom his own death in a personal sense, but can only muse that "This man apparently has not long to live" (VII, 16).

The rest of "A Boring Story" shows just how far the professor's life is from that which one would expect of the bearer of such an illustrious name. Chekhov dramatizes Nikolai Stepanovich's failure in human relationships by introducing several people who are part of his daily life. His lack of response to them reflects the bankruptcy of his emotions. His wife timidly tiptoes into the room "as if by accident" (VII, 17). This habit of hers is apparently the result of constant fear of disturbing her husband, as well as his inaccessibility to her. Their conversation lacks any element of a true dialogue: she speaks only about domestic drudgery, their daughter, their son, and the money they owe the servants, while he merely "listens and automatically says yes to everything" (VII, 17). However, Nikolai Stepanovich's wife is not the vulgarly calculating wife of Ivan Ilich. Nikolai Stepanovich recalls that he fell in love with her for her "good and clear mind, for her pure soul, for her beauty," and for her sympathy with his life. The professor's callousness and detachment caused his young bride, with all her possibilities, to develop into a clumsy old woman with a dull expression, who could only smile at cheap prices. How many times had he similarly stared off into space while she spoke, preoccupied with his own thoughts?

The professor admits that he cannot communicate with his daughter either. When she had been a child, he was able to buy her ice cream, to caress her, and to kiss her fingers, but he never learned to treat her as a thinking and feeling human being. Any efforts by his family to make him acknowledge their independent existence cause the professor to become uncomfortable.

The scene changes as he goes off to his "dear boys" (*milye mal'chiki*). We have seen Nikolai Stepanovich's failure as a husband

and father, we now learn of his success as a lecturer. This does not mean, however, that he communicates any better with medical students. His affection is not for his students, or for any particular student, but rather it is for an abstract and undifferentiated mass of students. He substitutes this love of the imaginary for genuine emotion.

The word "lecture," which is repeated ten times on a single page, punctuates his narration, sets its rhythm, and becomes a leitmotif carrying this notion. The "dear boys" now become a "many-headed serpent" (VII, 23), an object of conquest, not of love. Nikolai Stepanovich wants to influence, to teach, to control the mass of students, treating the lecture as a perfectly balanced work of art. At the same time the repetition of "passion" and "passionately" makes clear that lecturing is a substitute for sex as well, and perhaps the epithet "serpent" is no accident. The two sentences closing this particular segment of the first chapter indicate that:

Only during the lecture could I give myself up to passion, and understand that inspiration is not an invention of poets, but that it actually exists. And I think that Hercules after his most piquant exploit did not feel such a delightful exhaustion (*sladostnoe iznemozhenie*) as I experienced every time after a lecture. (VII, 24)

These long, flowing sentences are then succeeded by a curt "This was before" (VII, 24). The statement that he can no longer lecture well is like an admission of impotence, and it reintroduces the theme of death into the narrative. Left hollow by the loss of his passionate prowess, Nikolai Stepanovich begins to doubt that he ever truly loved teaching.

This presentation of Nikolai Stepanovich's academic life is enriched by the description of two characters who provide points of contrast to the professor. Nikolai the doorman does not esteem science but genuinely loves the university world:

If you want to know in what year someone defended his dissertation, joined the university staff, retired, or died, you have only to draw on the vast memory of this veteran, and he will tell you the year, the month, and the day, and will further supply you with every detail of the circumstances accompanying the event. His is the memory of one who loves. (VII, 20 - 21)

The professor describes his namesake as: "a scholar masked as a soldier, the guardian of university traditions. If the educated public loved science, learned men, and students as Nikolai does, our literature would long ago have been enriched by epics, biographies, and sayings, all of which, unfortunately, it now lacks" (VII, 21).

On the other hand, Nikolai Stepanovich (VII, 21) next meets his assistant, Petr Ignatevich, "a soldier masked as a scholar" (VII, 21). The professor points out his assistant's "fanatical faith in the infallibility of science and, above all, in anything written in German," and is curious as to "how this dry stick sleeps with his wife" (VII, 22). However, Petr Ignatevich's pedantry and dryness are only an exaggeration of the same tendencies in his superior. We have already seen the professor's devotion to science, heard that he only reads works written in German or English, and observed his superficial relationship with his own wife. Petr Ignatevich's inability to come to terms with death also mirrors Nikolai Stepanovich's failure in this regard. When told that Professor Perov has died, Petr Ignatevich's response is: "What was his field?" (*A chto on chital?*; VII, 22)

The second chapter continues to expose the weaknesses in Nikolai Stepanovich's personal and professional life. He is visited by a colleague whose entrance is reminiscent of the professor's wife: "I've only come for a minute, only a minute" (VII, 25). They have nothing of value to say to one another, so they pass the time with hollow pleasantries and forced laughter. The professor's reaction to the conversation is: "When at last I return to my room, my face goes on smiling—from inertia, I suppose" (VII, 26).

The next caller is a particularly lazy, ingratiating student who has failed the professor's exams five times. He begs Nikolai Stepanovich to give him a passing mark but the latter remains firm and ironic:

Of course, it won't make you any more erudite to take my examination another fifteen times, but it will develop your character. That's something to be thankful for. (VII, 27)

A third encounter is with a doctoral candidate who has come to request a topic for his dissertation. Nikolai Stepanovich explodes. He asks the young man why he cannot think of his own topic, rages at such a lack of self-esteem, and finally gives in:

He gets his theme from me, though it's not worth much, writes—under my supervision—a dissertation that will be of no use to anyone, and defends it in a dreary debate to receive a degree that will be of no use to him. (VII, 28)

Seeing him thus as professional, teacher, and counselor, we witness the poverty of Nikolai Stepanovich's beloved world of science.

His next visitor is the one person for whom the old man professes love: his ward, Katya. At the present time she lives in a house near his and visits him every day, content to sit quietly nearby while he works. Flashbacks show their relationship over the years. The professor speaks of her trusting nature, and of her devotion to him. In return she receives the usual detachment from Nikolai Stepanovich:

More than once I saw something taken away from her, saw her unjustly punished or her curiosity left unsatisfied; at such times a look of sadness mingled with the invariable expression of confidence in her face—but that was all. I did not know how to defend her, but when I saw her sadness, I felt like drawing her close to me and consoling her like an old nurse: "my dear little orphan!" (VII, 29)

Instead, when Katya would come to share some experience with him that filled her with elation, he would point to the clock and say, "I'll give you half an hour—go ahead" (VII, 29).

Katya left the professor's home to become an actress. She experienced professional failure, an unhappy love affair, and the death of her child, but to each of these crises Nikolai Stepanovich who "loved her like a daughter," only "wrote long boring letters which I didn't have to write at all" (VII, 32 - 33). Katya aptly described Nikolai Stepanovich's unwillingness to communicate as follows:

The best men view this evil only from a distance, not caring to come closer, instead of taking one's part, write heavy-handed commonplaces and utterly superfluous sermons . . . . (VII, 32)

She continued to love Nikolai Stepanovich as a father, however, and, after she had to accept her lack of talent, Katya returned to him.

Following this description of Katya, the chapter concludes with Nikolai Stepanovich again facing his alienation from his family. His daughter is being courted by Gnekker, a shallow, rather vulgar man, whom he cannot stand. It is clear that Gnekker will take over the household when the old man dies, and the reason he will succeed him so easily is that Nikolai Stepanovich never really occupied the position in the first place.

Chapter 3 focuses on the professor's and Katya's relationship as it is in the present. Their conversation begins with Nikolai Stepanovich's advice to Katya: "You should occupy yourself with something," or "You ought to get married" (VII, 39). He then indulges in a long, self-pitying speech:

I am no longer a king. Something worthy only of a slave is going on inside me: evil thoughts prowl through my mind day and night, and my soul is a hotbed of feelings such as I have never known before. . . What is the meaning of this? If these thoughts and feelings have arisen from a change in my convictions, then what has caused the change? Can the world have grown worse and I better, or is it that I have been blind till now, and indifferent? If the change results from general decline of my mental and physical powers—I am a sick man, you know, losing weight every day—then my situation is indeed pitiable: it means my new ideas are abnormal, morbid, that I ought to be ashamed of them and consider them of no importance . . . . (VII, 40)

Katya argues that this change in the professor is actually a revelation: he can no longer deny the sterility of his life. She begs him to leave his family, to make a clean break once and for all, and live out his days in peace. When he falls back upon his supposed obligation to the university, that part of his existence comes under attack as well:

Give that up too. What's the university to you? It makes no sense. You've been lecturing there for thirty years, and where are your students now? How many of them are well-known scientists? Just count them! It doesn't require a good and talented man to increase the number of doctors who exploit ignorance and pile up hundreds of thousands of rubles for themselves. You are not needed. (VII, 41)

Taken aback by Katya's words, which call into question what he had always considered an eminently successful life, Nikolai Stepanovich hastens to change the subject.

Chapter 5 dramatizes one of those long nights when the insomniac professor is plagued by "new and evil feelings." His physical condition, the sounds he hears, and the flickering of a candle seem to tell him that he will die. However, Nikolai Stepanovich is in no way prepared for death, and he feels as capable as Ivan Ilich of screaming out his indignation over the meaninglessness of life: "Ki-vi! Ki-vi! A screech suddenly pierced the silence of the night and I could not tell whether it came from outside or from within my breast. Ki-vi! Ki-vi!" (VII, 56). Death is pursuing him with flickering shadows, howling dogs, and above all with his recent discovery of the existential void, and Nikolai Stepanovich can muster no defense. He feels nothing but terror.

This terror soon reveals itself as another manifestation of Nikolai Stepanovich's self-preoccupation. His wife comes and begs him to comfort his daughter, who for some reason is hysterically upset. He goes to Liza's room convinced that he will die at any moment. His daughter throws herself into his arms, crying out her need for him, while his wife stands beside him, helping as much as she can. In short, they are finally together as a real family. However, this state lasts but a second. Not comprehending the cause of Liza's distress, Nikolai Stepanovich instinctively steps back and analyzes the situation in his own terms:

"It's nonsense," I thought, "the influence of one organism upon another." My violent, nervous tension communicated itself to my wife, to Liza, to the dog, that's all . . . . This sort of transference explains prescience and foreboding. (VII, 57)

Once again Nikolai Stepanovich fails to recognize his daughter's independent existence. He interprets her misery only as a function of his own depression.

Indifference, which has characterized the professor throughout the story, assumes the role of a verbal leitmotif in the final chapter. Nikolai Stepanovich's indifference consists mainly of his desire never to deviate from the path that he has set before him. He relies upon his consciousness to put things into perspective, but then never acts upon his judgment. He is content to observe events passively, and to let life take its course.

Nikolai Stepanovich has accepted the consciousness of his indifference as a revelation and not as an aberration, but he decides that any major personality change would be ridiculous at this stage. If his life cannot be the beautifully wrought work of art he has always dreamed of, at least he will guarantee its appearing so:

Since it would have been useless and indeed beyond my strength to struggle against my present mood, I have determined that the last days of my life should be irreproachable, at least outwardly. If I have been wrong where my family is concerned, which I am well aware is the case, then I will try to do what they wish. I am asked to go to Kharkov—I go to Kharkov. Besides, I have grown so indifferent to everything of late that it does not matter to me where I go . . . . (VII, 58)

Yet in this same chapter the leitmotif "name" reappears in its pejorative connotation. Nikolai Stepanovich ostensibly deplores the separation of "name" and "reality":

Great names are apparently created to live a life of their own, apart from those who bear them. At this moment my name is nonchalantly parading about Kharkov; in another three months, set old in bold letters on my tombstone, it will blaze like the sun itself—while I shall be covered with moss. (VII, 61)

Is this split of the professor's own choosing? Celebrated names are not created without the participation of the one who bears the name. As we have seen above, Nikolai Stepanovich wants above all to maintain the integrity of his reputation, his outward reality. So beneath the indifferent narrative of "A Boring Story" we must seek a consciousness which, through this confessional monologue, attempts to secure its good name, to make his life appear as the work of art that it never was.

This is what Chekhov had in mind when he deplored a conscious life without a world-view, which means a concern for one's neighbors. Life is not a beautiful composition to be conceived and executed according to an *a priori* plan. In order to live, one must be willing to face the unexpected, to change, to become vulnerable, to know what it means to be hurt and to be happy. A straight line is a boring road. Living requires imagination, that is, the ability to project outside of one's known experience. As Katya astutely observes, imagination is something that Nikolai Stepanovich does not have.

One might argue that Nikolai Stepanovich does indeed have a goal in life: the advancement of science. When all faith in his existence has departed, the love of science still remains:

Now, on the threshold of death, the only thing that interests me is what interested me twenty or thirty years ago—science. Even as I breathe my last, I shall go on believing that science is the most important, most beautiful, most essential thing in the life of man, that it always has been and always will be the highest manifestation of love, that by means of it alone will man conquer nature and himself. (VII, 24)

Nikolai Stepanovich regards science in terms of his self-image as a scientist.

As far as we can tell, Nikolai Stepanovich was a good and conscientious scientist, and whatever his motivation, he probably made significant contributions to medical study. We cannot see the fruit of these endeavors. We do see, however, that he has also assumed the role of husband, father, and friend. He will not reject these roles, but neither will he recognize the demands they place upon him.

The development of this theme culminates in the final chapter. Nikolai Stepanovich is in Kharkov where he hopes to gather information on Gnekker's family. As he sits in his hotel room engrossed in his usual self-contemplation, Katya suddenly arrives, and begs him to advise her what she should do with her life:

"Help me!" she sobs, seizing my hand and kissing it. "After all you are my father, my only friend! And you are wise, educated. You have lived a long time! You have been a teacher! Tell me: what am I to do?" (VII, 62)

Nikolai Stepanovich has no ready answer for her and so, as with his daughter Liza, he tries to change the subject. She persists, however, and he shrinks back:

"What a queer girl you are, really," I mutter, "I don't understand . . . Such a sensible girl, and suddenly you . . . go off into tears!" Silence. (VII, 62 - 63)

Katya had always loved the professor for his wisdom, and had hoped that she could perhaps share in and benefit from his clear vision, but at last she realizes that there is no sympathy in him. She quits him forever, and the old man loses the one person who cared for him, and for whom he felt love. The greater tragedy is that Katya has changed. She fails to respond when he tells her that he will soon be dead. In the final few paragraphs the once-vibrant girl is depicted by the repetition of "dry and cold." Nikolai Stepanovich himself observes that "the soul of this poor creature has never found and never in her life will find refuge . . . never in her life!" (VII, 63).

Admittedly, Nikolai Stepanovich could not tell Katya how to make her life meaningful, but had he perhaps shown more concern and compassion toward her, she may have felt a reason to exist. Instead she is met with aloofness. It seems that Chekhov believed the professor to be responsible for Katya's deterioration, a sentiment he expressed in a letter to Pleshcheyev (September 30, 1889):

My hero—and this is one of his chief characteristics, is altogether too indifferent to the inner life of those around him. At a time when people near him are crying, blundering through life and lying, he pontificates calmly about the theater and literature. Had he been different, Liza and Katya probably would not have perished.[5]

Nikolai Stepanovich cannot change, Liza marries Gnekker, and Katya heads toward the Caucasus for further disillusionment.

Nikolai Stepanovich is not so simple to catalogue, however. Chekhov himself admitted that he could not keep the story under strict control: "There are fifteen moods in my story, not two," and anyone who has read "A Boring Story" cannot help but agree. We have examined the professor in terms of the negative consequences of his indifference, but in many ways he is an admirable figure. At one point Katya refers to his complexity in the following manner: "You are a rare specimen. The actor doesn't exist who could play you. Even a poor actor could play me, for instance, or Mikhail Feodorych, but not you." (VII, 53).

He strives to abide by the dictum "Know thyself," and regards himself honestly, recognizing his own banality and dullness. Nikolai Stepanovich is truly wise in the sense of one who sees through life's illusions and puts things into perspective. However, this balanced objectivity is a detriment in that it shields the professor from life and prevents him from responding personally to those around him.

"A Boring Story" is almost tragic in its depiction of a man unable to externalize his inner world. The old man cannot find the means to express what he feels; he finds himself dumb when he wishes most to speak. His every thought comes out as a platitude, meaningless and boring. Those tender thoughts which the reader witnesses, such as the final words, "farewell, my precious!" (VII, 63) are never heard by the persons for whom they are intended. Thus, like Katya, we sense the professor's inner goodness, and we feel warm toward him at the same time that we grow impatient.

For Nikolai Stepanovich truly suffers. He feels that he is losing his admirable qualities of judgment and restraint, and now, as he reevaluates his life in terms of impending death, he sees that his accomplishments have not satisfied his expectations. Nevertheless, he does not hide behind his name or rationalize away his situation. Paradoxically, the old man becomes increasingly more alive, increasingly more aware, the more certain he becomes that he understands nothing.

In the end we are confronted with more than the life of this man. We are faced with a kind of cosmic paralysis: "Can one live fully conscious of the shortcomings around him, capable of seeing things as they truly are, and still communicate and relate to his neighbors?" Or, putting it in Dostoevskian terms, "Can one transcend the underground?" Nikolai Stepanovich has no answer to the dilemma. If Chekhov has one, he does not give it.

One reason for the ambivalence of the professor's character lies in the peculiar relationship between Nikolai Stepanovich and his creator. When the story first appeared in 1889, among others, Suvorin recognized the parallels between Nikolai Stepanovich and the Chekhov he knew. Chekhov denied this allegation vehemently: "When one serves you coffee, do not think to find beer in it. When I offer you a professor's ideas, trust me, and do not search in them for Chekhov's ideas. Throughout the entire story there is only one idea with which I agree—the one that comes to the mind of the swindler, Gnekker, the professor's son-in-law: 'The old man is in his dotage.' All the rest is invented and artificial" (to Suvorin, October 17, 1889).[6]

However, Suvorin's observation is not unfounded. Both Chekhov and Nikolai Stepanovich retained a love of science, yet neither chose to devote himself to the practice of medicine. Chekhov instinctively reacted to life and people by stepping back and watching from afar, a feature of his personality that he strove to overcome. Also, he shared the professor's ability to see through illusions. Chekhov's characterization of Nikolai Stepanovich is marked by a desire to show the results of that indifference which he himself knew well, and at the same time by a deeply rooted perhaps unconscious sympathy. We know that at the time Chekhov was searching hard for a path in life. His creation of Nikolai Stepanovich taught him what he must avoid, and the next year in April, 1890, he left for Sakhalin. This long and arduous journey had no literary motivations whatsoever, but was rather a strictly scientific and humanitarian project. Chekhov did medical and social research on the island, compiling information on notecards that was eventually expanded into a book, *Sakhalin Island,* published in 1893. The book had some effect toward initiating long-called-for reforms in the penal colony, and its publication partially fulfilled Chekhov's initial commitment to medicine. Chekhov himself said of the book that he was glad such a "rough convict's smock will hang in my literary wardrobe."

Chekhov spent approximately three months on the island, from July to October, 1890, and then left aboard a steamer bound for Odessa. En route to Russia he visited Hong Kong, Singapore, and Ceylon, which he loved, and wrote a short story, "Gusev," that was influenced by the sea voyage.

II "Gusev" *December, 1890*

"Gusev" was begun in Ceylon on November 12 of 1890, and it speaks far more eloquently than any didactic work could. As in "Lights" there is a dramatic confrontation between two opposing types of men. In this story the unreflecting man of nature is contrasted with the conscious individual who protests against life's injustice. The story is composed of five short sections, like the five acts of a drama. In the first act the protagonists are introduced and the conflict defined by their dialogue. The second act deepens and clarifies the main theme by showing the different ways in which Gusev and Pavel Ivanych perceive reality. The third centers on Pavel Ivanych and gives an idea of his existence beyond the immediate circumstances. The fourth act describes the death of Pavel Ivanych and Gusev's preparation for death. In the fifth act the death, funeral, and "afterlife" of Gusev are given. Chekhov heightens the dramatic mode by employing an objective narrator who makes comments of his own.

The story begins with Gusev, a discharged orderly, speaking to Pavel Ivanych, "a man of uncertain social status" (VII, 77). They are aboard a ship traveling from the Far East to Russia, and at the moment are in unbearably hot Oriental waters. The men are lying in the ship's infirmary, and are evidently soon to die, a sentiment which the very first words of the story suggest: "It is already dark, it will soon be night" (VII, 77). Gusev speaks of a giant fish that will rip a hole in the ship's bottom, and refers to the wind as a great beast that escaped its chains. These ignorant superstitions irritate the dying Pavel Ivanych, and he upbraids Gusev because he does not think for himself.

The conversation is interrupted as Gusev slips into a delirium transporting him to his home, which he has not seen in five years. He gazes upon dear faces, and happily feels himself a part of the simple, domestic scenes. Suddenly, for no reason at all, this vision is replaced by that of a huge bull's head with no eyes and clouds of black smoke. This nightmare does not bother Gusev though; he is simply happy to have been able to see "his people."

The conversation between the two men resumes. Pavel Ivanych expresses indignation over the fact that Gusev was placed on the ship despite his illness; that, in fact, he was sent away to die. Gusev cannot understand what the other man is talking about. He thinks that he is being reproached for becoming ill, and replies that he lay on the ship's deck the night he caught a chill simply because he had no strength. Pavel Ivanych rails against the manner in which Gusev's life has been wasted:

Yes, very good! The lieutenant drafts plans all day long, and you sit in the kitchen and long for home . . . Plans, indeed! . . . It's not plans that matter but human life. You have only one life to live and it mustn't be wronged. (VII, 80)

Gusev does not understand this either. It has never occurred to him to want anything out of life, or even to expect anything but living.

In a letter to Suvorin, Chekhov makes a claim which may well be applied to Gusev: "You asked me in your last letter, 'What should a Russian man desire?' Here is my answer: to desire. He needs most of all, desire, temperament." Gusev, the passive Russian peasant, seemingly has no desires. Yet the resentment that Pavel Ivanych (and probably Chekhov) would like Gusev to feel, does express itself unconsciously. His happy dreams are continually supplanted by the image of the sightless bull, the subconscious embodiment of blind, brute force. It is as if Gusev's unconscious knows that he will never see his home again, recognizing that return is frustrated by a power beyond his control. Gusev's repressed bitterness also revealed itself when he beat up four Chinese laborers for no other reason than boredom and their helplessness. One recalls the early story "Small Fry" in which Nevyrazimov, feeling himself crushed by life, kills the one creature even more helpless than he, a cockroach.

Nevertheless, Gusev has an affinity with the world. A living creature, he is a brother to the animals and his fellow man. He gives himself up to immanent sensation, and is perfectly comfortable in the world. When Stepan, a soldier, lies down on the floor to rest, Gusev knows automatically that the man is dead. He expresses anger only because the other men do not see this and try to revive him. Pavel Ivanych on the other hand refers to himself as "a personified protest," a man who will never accept injustice. He declares that he will travel to Kharkov to give a writer-friend of his an inflammatory account of Gusev's abuse. However, as a "conscious" man who wants to shine the light of inquiry upon everything, the dying Pavel Ivanych ironically deludes himself with the hope of his own recovery. His last thoughts are of the thievery that Gusev's officer must have engaged in. His "protest" strikes the reader as pathetic, for he dies just as suddenly and undramatically as the soldier.

Gusev's understanding of reality includes a natural belief in the afterworld as taught by his peers. When a sailor asks him if Pavel Ivanych will go to Heaven, Gusev answers affirmatively and explains: "He will . . . He suffered so long. Then again, he belonged to the clergy and priests have a lot of relatives. Their prayers will get him there" (VII, 84). He is able to communicate easily with this sailor, who tells him that he will die soon. The thought of death fills Gusev with a "vague craving" (VII, 85). He asks the sailor to take him onto the deck where he can breathe fresh air. He gets no relief there, though. The air is heavy and oppressive, and he perceives a variation of his nightmare of the blind bull:

The sea has neither sense nor pity. If the steamer had been smaller, not made of thick iron plates, the waves would have crushed it without distinguishing between saints and sinners. The steamer's expression was equally senseless and cruel. This beaked monster presses forward, cutting millions of waves in its path; it fears neither darkness nor the wind, nor space, nor solitude—it's all child's play for it, and if the ocean had its population, this monster would crush it, too, without distinguishing between saints and sinners. (VII, 86)

The image of the sightless bull's head has been raised to a cosmic plane in this description of a hostile and menacing universe. Yet Gusev does not reason any of this. He simply regrets that he won't be able to rejoin his family.

Gusev's death is never reported. "He was sleeping for two days and on the third at noon two sailors come down and carry him out of the infirmary" (VII, 86). Chekhov does not refer to "Gusev's body," he continues to call it Gusev. Thus, when the body is thrown into the sea, the story reads: "Gusev slides off it slowly and then flying, head foremost, turns over in the air and—plop!" (VII, 87). There is little difference in Gusev alive or dead. That he never "wakes up" from his sleep only further reaffirms Gusev's organic bond with the world, but even at the bottom of the ocean he finds no peace: his body is attacked by a shark. Meanwhile, above the surface of the sea, the setting sun creates a scene of extreme splendor.

If there is any reason to call Chekhov pessimistic, it is on account of this story. As in "Lights" we are not left with an intimation of the "right path" in life. Self-conscious man, unconscious peasant, both die and are thrown into the ocean like logs. The story ends with a vision of sunset, but it is clear that this incredible beauty has nothing to do with human destiny. Man receives only hostility, for dead men do not rise to the heavens; they sink to the depths of the terrible sea.

III   "The Duel" *1891*

"The Duel" was serialized in the periodical *Novoe vremya* in 1891. While Chekhov was writing the story he often met and talked with the zoologist Nikolai Wagner about the survival of the fittest, heredity, degeneration, and other topics which were in vogue at that time. Chekhov's position in these conversations was that the human spirit is capable of conquering the weaknesses of heredity and of overcoming certain character deficiencies. Of course, Chekhov was not speaking in a religious sense when he mentioned the "human spirit," but rather in the existential frame of reference that Albert Camus had in mind in *The Plague* when he wrote, "to state quite simply what we learn in time of pestilence: there are more things to admire in men than to despise." However, this particular story does not portray a great victory of the human spirit. Rather it deals with the kind of modest, unromantic self-knowledge in which man is capable of coming to terms with his own mediocrity, and accepting it.

The editor of *Novoe vremya* proposed that the title of this novelette should be changed from "The Duel" to "The Lie." However, Chekhov declined this suggestion replying:

For my story your title, "The Lie," is not a fitting one. It would have been fitting in a place where the lie is conscious. The unconscious lie is not a lie but an error.

Indeed, Chekhov's story places a much greater emphasis on unconscious self-deception and role playing than on the deliberate lying of his protagonist. Chekhov's intention in this story is to unmask those characters who are evading reality behind the cloak of ideology and whim, and he chooses the central incident of the duel to accomplish this.

The personality conflict between Von Koren and Laevsky is developed from the third chapter of the novelette, and culminates in the nineteenth chapter with the actual duel between the two men. The epiphany which follows the duel and its effects on the characters are dealt with in the last two chapters. It is interesting to note that each of these characters has an ideological predecessor in Chekhov's play *Ivanov* (1889): Laevsky is modeled after the ineffectual "superfluous man" Ivanov, and Von Koren, after the dogmatic, self-righteous Dr. Lvov.

The prosaic opening lines of "The Duel" create an atmosphere immediately:

It was eight in the morning—the time when the officers, local officials, and the visitors usually took their morning dip in the sea after the hot, stifling night, and then went to the pavilion to drink tea or coffee. (VII, 99)

Chekhov purposely does not begin the first chapter with a description of the majestic mountains or the beautiful sea, but rather he chooses this viewpoint because it accords with his character Laevsky's perception of the scene. Romanticism is further undercut in the next few paragraphs. Laevsky and Dr. Samoilenko are bathing in the sea, discussing Laevsky's hypothetical statement concerning the termination of a love affair, when a wave breaks over both of them.

After dressing and seating themselves in the pavilion, Laevsky and Samoilenko resume their conversation. Laevsky is established almost immediately as either a romantic or a pseudo-romantic by his statement: "We are crippled by civilization" (VII, 101). This cry was first uttered by Rousseau, and was later repeated by the leading art figures of the nineteenth century, including Tolstoi, who wore a medallion with Rousseau's portrait on it from the time he was fifteen years old.

Yet Laevsky proceeds to tell Samoilenko that the dreams he cherished of fleeing from civilization, and the new meaningful life he had envisaged in the Caucasus were all "self-deception." He had dreamed of this romantic ideal with Nadezhda Fedorovna, a married woman with whom he fled to the south, but now after two years he confesses that he has no intention of ever beginning a "life of labor and a vineyard." Moreover, Nadezhda's advanced education and feminine charms no longer have any appeal for Laevsky:

As for love, I ought to tell you that living with a woman who has read Spencer and has followed you to the ends of the earth is no more interesting than living with any Anfisa or Akulina. There's the same smell of ironing, powder and of medicines, the same curl-papers every morning, the same self-deception. (VII, 101 - 102)

To this the doctor replies, "You can't get along without an iron in a household." Obviously Samoilenko has totally failed to understand the disillusioned romanticism that Laevsky is trying to communicate to him, and he responds with advice that is consistent with his own values:

Love cannot last long. You have lived two years in love, and now evidently your married life has reached the point when, in order to preserve equilibrium, so to speak, you ought to exercise patience. (VII, 102)

The doctor's philosophy is rather simple: the best approach to an ethico-philosophical problem is to avoid it, to elevate patience above all, and to adopt a role that will not disturb the surface of the established routine.

The placid, prosaic character of the doctor is also conveyed with several other details in the subtext, which portray him much more vividly than the opening descriptive paragraphs. It is mentioned that Samoilenko has never read Tolstoi, and his mundane nature is further underlined by his sensual enjoyment of coffee, cognac, and ice water as he gazes out at the sea, after which he comments, "Remarkably splendid view" (VII, 100).

Nadezhda Feydorovna is first introduced through Laevsky's impression of her in chapter 3. When he returns to their apartment, Laevsky finds his mistress dressed, drinking coffee, and reading a thick magazine. His immediate reaction is that she is deliberately posing before him, and he is enraged by her pretensions. He looks at her neck with aversion, and recalls how in Tolstoi's novel Anna Karenina felt a similar disgust at her husband's ears. Laevsky's identification with Anna is ironical in this instance. It would seem that Nadezhda, who left her husband for Laevsky and very likely might be destroyed by him, would feel a much closer parallel to Anna's position. But there is another, more pervasive irony which runs throughout this chapter. It is only later that the reader learns that Nadezhda Fedorovna herself has become bored with Laevsky, and has already had an affair with the police captain, Kirilin.

In addition to Laevsky's extreme irritation with Nadezhda, chapter 2 also focuses on his desire to escape to St. Petersburg. Laevsky feels that all of his problems would immediately be solved if only he could somehow return to that city: an illusion which will later be echoed in Chekhov's *Three Sisters'* call, "To Moscow, to Moscow." The word *bezhat* (to run away) is nostalgically spoken eight times by Laevsky in this chapter, and it repeatedly draws attention to his inability to face reality.

Laevsky is understandably guilt-ridden at the thought of abandoning his mistress, and chides himself that there is no "guiding principle" in his life. He forces himself to be saccharinely polite to Nadezhda, calling her "golubka" (darling) rather than expressing his true feelings. He concludes that his psychological conflicts and indecision are very similar to those suffered by Hamlet. Yet this literary allusion also is not without irony. In chapter 1 Laevsky is described with a sufficient number of mundane details to make a comparison between himself and the lofty, regal Hamlet comic. Laevsky gnaws at his fingernails, shuffles his feet, and wears loose slippers over badly darned socks!

In chapters 3 and 4 Laevsky's ideological antagonist the zoologist Von Koren is introduced. Von Koren's aggressive personality and his vanity are conveyed in the opening description of him as habitually admiring his swarthy good looks in the mirror, and aiming his pistol at a prince's portrait in Samoilenko's parlor. The latter detail foreshadows Von Koren's role as an instigator in the forthcoming duel.

The dynamics of the conflict between Laevsky and Von Koren are developed in this chapter with the psychological portrait the scientist draws of Laevsky and his brutal reaction to it. Hatred has indeed sharpened Von Koren's appreciation of his opponent's faults, and he is convinced that "To drown him [Laevsky] would be a service." However, Von Koren is careful to justify his personal criticism of Laevsky with that man's negative sociological and genetic influences on other people:

I should have passed him by if he were not so noxious and dangerous. His noxiousness lies first of all in the fact that he has great success with women and so threatens to leave descendants—that is, to present the world with a dozen Laevskys as feeble and depraved as himself. Secondly, he is in the highest degree contaminating. I have spoken to you already of vint and beer. In another year or two he will dominate the whole Caucasian coast . . . . In the interests of humanity and in their own interests, such people ought to be destroyed. (VII, 115 - 116)

In chapters 6 and 7 all the characters congregate at an evening picnic where relationships between them are further defined. Von Koren disagrees with and insults Laevsky at every opportunity, and the latter is afraid and embarrassed by this. Nadezhda Fedorovna is in a flirtatious, lighthearted mood, and throughout the chapter there are descriptions of her feelings of flight:

She wanted to skip and jump, to laugh, to shout, to tease, to flirt . . . . She seemed to herself little, simple, light, ethereal as a butterfly. (VII, 128)

Nadezhda's flighty mood makes her impervious to the threats of her jilted lover Kirilin, whose warning advice to her is: "I venture to assure you I am a gentleman, and I don't allow anyone to doubt it. Adieu!" (VII, 130) She is much more involved in her new interest in Achmianov, the shopkeeper's young and handsome son:

If she, for instance, were to turn the head of this handsome young fool! How amusing, absurd, wild it would be really! And she suddenly felt a longing to make him love her, plunder him, throw him over, and then to see what would come of it. (VII, 130)

Nadezhda's mood shifts rapidly when she is upbraided by Laevsky for being a coquette, and she immediately feels "heavy, stout, coarse, and drunk" (VII, 132). This depression deepens when later at home Nadezhda is presented with a letter bearing the news of her husband's death, and she sobs like a child to Laevsky, "What a sin, what a sin! Save me, Vanya, save me . . . . I have been mad . . . . I am lost" (VII, 134).

However, Laevsky is thinking only of escape, and in his desperation crawls out of a window to seek asylum at Samoilenko's house. He begs his friend for a loan to return to St. Petersburg, and in a shaking voice which recalls Nadezhda's plea to him a short while before he begs: "Save me! I beseech you, I implore you" (VII, 134). Samoilenko agrees to help Laevsky, who, as in the first chapter, reminds him of a "weak, defenseless child."

In the ensuing conversation with Samoilenko, Laevsky weaves between lies and truth, which in his jubilant mood he doesn't distinguish. He declares joyfully that he will send for Nadezhda after he has reached St. Petersburg, although he has no intention of doing this. There follows a very astute judgment of Von Koren's despotic character, and a confession which is not totally sincere:

I am a foolish, worthless, depraved man. The air I breathe, this wine, love, life in fact—for all that, I have given nothing in exchange so far but lying, idleness, cowardice, till now I have deceived myself and other people . . . I'm glad I see my faults clearly and am conscious of them. That will help me become a different man. My dear fellow, if you only knew how passionately, with what anguish, I long for such a change. (VII, 137)

Later, when upon Von Koren's insistence, Samoilenko stipulates that Laevsky must send Nadezhda on to St. Petersburg before him, Laevsky is terrified to think that perhaps the doctor has detected his deception:

He began to understand that he would need deception not only in the remote future, but today, and tomorrow, and in a month's time, and perhaps up to the very end of his life . . . He would have to lie to Nadezhda Fedorovna, to his creditors, and to his superiors in the service . . . . he would have to resort to a regular series of deceptions, little and big, in order to get free of her . . . . Deception and nothing more. (VII, 151)

Laevsky is not the only character who is snared in the mesh of deception. Three days after the picnic a neighborhood gossip with "a bittersweet expression" comes to "console" Nadezhda Fedorovna on the death of her husband, and to recommend strongly that she marry Laevsky. Nadezhda is not so anxious to be saved as she was a few nights before, and besides she doesn't want to marry Laevsky in view of her relations with Kirilin and Achmianov. Her neighbor responds with a series of harsh truths about Nadezhda's immoral, "unclear" behavior. Nadezhda finds the deprecating remarks about her clothes the most shocking revelation, as "she had always had the highest opinion of her costumes" (VII, 141). However, she is also visibly moved by her neighbor's criticism of her unwifely, coquettish behavior. She feels thoroughly chastened and decides that her only recourse is to escape to Russia where she will "do a translation . . . . or open a library" (VII, 142). Nadezhda says nothing of her plans to Laevsky, and their mutual deceit further develops the irony introduced in chapter two. Later that night at the very same party where Laevsky is unmasked by the doctor's stipulation to his loan, Nadezhda is brutally awakened from her reveries of moral regeneration. She is musing how she "would live in some far remote place . . . and send Laevsky 'anonymously' money, embroidered shirts and tobacco, and would return to him only in his old age or if he were dangerously ill and needed a nurse" (VII, 152), when she receives a note from Kirilin: "If you don't give me an interview today, I shall take measures" (VII, 152).

The dramatic pace of the novelette accelerates from this point as Laevsky and Nadezhda are confronted with both their own and other people's deceptions. The police chief, Kirilin, is furious that Nadezhda has wearied of him after only two rendezvous, and feels that his honor has been impugned. He demands to meet with her that night and the next, or else he threatens to create a scandal. Nedezhda complies, forgetting her previous engagement for that evening with Achmianov, who thinks, "It's deceit, deceit . . ." (VII, 157).

The following morning Laevsky heads toward Samoilenko's, having already decided that he will lie "not all at once, but piecemeal" (VII, 157). However, Laevsky is met with a rude shock when he finds Von Koren there, and he becomes increasingly irritated by that man's hostile remarks. When Von Koren mentions that he is well aware of Laevsky's present position and considers it "hopeless," Laevsky can no longer control himself. He vents his anger on Samoilenko, who has just entered, and is ignorant of the preceding conversation.

At this point Laevsky self-righteously considers that he has been deceived by the doctor, whom he accuses of gossiping about his private affairs. Samoilenko is offended, an argument ensues, but Von Koren resolves it with the statement,

Now we understand . . . Mr. Laevsky wants to amuse himself with a duel before he goes away. I can give him that pleasure. Mr. Laevsky, I accept your challenge. (VII, 160)

The night before the duel is painful and terrifying for Laevsky. The surge of confidence he had felt earlier that afternoon vanishes as the sun goes down:

It was dread at the thought of something unknown. He knew that the night would be long and sleepless, and that he would have to think not only of

Von Koren and his hatred, but also of the mountain of lies which he had to get through, and which he had not the ability to dispense with. (VII, 162)

The first lie which Laevsky is confronted with is not his own, but rather that of his mistress, Nadezhda. Motivated by jealous revenge, the "deceived" Achmianov leads Laevsky to the hotel where Kirilin and Nadezhda are meeting for their second night together.

The knowledge of Nadezhda's deceit jars Laevsky from his mood of terrified anxiety to a painful acceptance of his situation. In the night that follows, Laevsky admits all his former deceits, including the illusion that escaping to St. Petersburg would redeem him: "He must look for salvation in himself alone, and if there were no finding it, why waste time? He must kill himself, that was all" (VII, 171).

Significantly, a storm arises during this night of revelation with violent gusts of wind and flashes of lightning that parallel the spiritual crisis Laevsky is passing through. As it begins to get light, the storm subsides and the carriage that will take Laevsky to the duel arrives. Before he leaves, however, Laevsky embraces the repentant Nadezhda, who he realizes is "the one creature near and dear to him, whom no one could replace" (VII, 172). Laevsky has finally understood the meaning and beauty in reality as it is, and "when he went out of the house and got into the carriage he wanted to return home alive" (VII, 172).

Von Koren arrives late at the designated spot for the duel, and comments upon the beauty of the rising sun:

"It's the first time in my life I've seen it! How glorious!" said Von Koren, pointing to the glade and stretching out his hands to the east. "Look, green rays." (VII, 175)

His lines recall Pechorin's speech in Mikhail Lermontov's *A Hero of Our Time* before the duel with Grushnitsky:

I do not remember a bluer and fresher morning. The sun had just appeared from behind the green summits, and the merging of the first warmth of its rays with the waning coolness of the night pervaded all one's senses with a kind of delicious languor.[7]

It would seem that the parallel between these passages was created intentionally by Chekhov, especially in view of Pechorin's description of his feelings before the duel:

Out of life's storm I carried only a few ideas—and not one feeling. For a long time now I have been living not with the heart, but with the head.[8]

This similarity between Von Koren and Pechorin is ironical in that they differ radically in their personal philosophies. However, their conceit and their cold aloofness unite them at a very essential point. Von Koren's identification with Pechorin also gives an indication that he will have the upper hand in the forthcoming duel, which will indeed be the case.

In contrast to Von Koren's bold excitement, Laevsky is in a state of exhaustion and nervous agitation before the duel. His estrangement is reflected in his stiff, awkward walk, which causes the deacon to compare him with an old man, and in his desire "to be killed as soon as possible or taken home" (VII, 176).

The duel itself parodies famous descriptions of such confrontations in Russian literature. No one present has ever witnessed a duel, and there is an initial doubt as to procedure. Von Koren laughs and says, "Gentlemen, who remembers the description in Lermontov? In Turgenev, too, Bazarov had a duel with someone . . . ." (VII, 178) Laevsky magnanimously fires into the air, and Von Koren prepares to kill his hated opponent as Pechorin did in *A Hero of Our Time*, when the deacon shouts, "He'll kill him!" The shot intended for Laevsky just grazes his neck, and the entire event ends on a comic note.

His ridiculous duel is the turning point of the story. After it, Laevsky returns home to be reconciled with Nadezhda Fedorovna and to begin a new life with her. He permanently abandons his romantic illusions, and accepts a mediocre life of constant work and frugality.

Von Koren and Laevsky are also reconciled. The last chapter describes Von Koren's departure from the town in uncertain, stormy weather. Chekhov purposely uses this description to underline Von Koren's increased awareness of the uncertainties in life, which even scientific knowledge cannot always predict. Von Koren bids farewell to Laevsky and admits:

I was mistaken in regard to you, but it's easy to make a false step even on a smooth road, and in fact, it's the natural human lot: if one is not mistaken in the main, one is mistaken in the details. (VII, 183)

At the end of "The Duel" both Laevsky and Von Koren have met the impact of reality and adjusted their philosophy to its demands.

Both realize that neither science nor the human imagination is the ruling force of the universe, and there is a resemblance between their last words that unites the two men, as well as expressing the theme of the story. "There is no such thing as truth . . ." says Laevsky, reaffirming Von Koren's comment that "it's easy to make a false step even on a smooth road," and eloquently stating both his own and the general human condition (VII, 185).

IV "Ward Number Six" 1892

Like "The Duel," "Ward Number Six" is developed as a philosophical polemic between two contrasting characters. However, the elements of social protest that were perhaps influenced by Chekhov's journey to Sakhalin are much more prominent than in any of his earlier works. Shortly after "Ward Number Six" was published in 1892 Chekhov wrote Suvorin a letter which indicates a shift in his attitude toward the artist's role:

Remember that those whom we call "immortal," or simply good writers, and who intoxicate us, have one most important feature in common: they are going somewhere, and are calling us there, and one feels not with one's mind, but with one's whole being, that they have some goal, like the ghost of Hamlet's father, which didn't come and stir up people's imagination just to pass the time of day. Some of them—it depends on their calibre—have immediate aims: serfdom, the liberation of their country, politics, beauty or simply vodka . . . . others have distant aims like God, the life hereafter, human happiness and so on. The best of them are realists and describe life as it is, but because every line that they write is saturated with the consciousness of a goal, one senses, in addition to life as it is, life as it should be, and that grips one. (Nov. 25, 1892)[9]

There are many theories as to what Chekhov's "goal" really was in this work. A common interpretation has been to conceive of it as a refutation of Tolstoiism. Chekhov's renunciation of this philosophy is a well-known fact, which can be supported by his later works as well as by a letter written in 1894:

Tolstoi's philosophy affected me powerfully and held me in its grip for about six or seven years . . . But now something in me protests; reason and justice tell me that there is more love for humanity in electricity and steam than in chastity and in abstention from meat. War is an evil, and law-courts are an evil—but that doesn't mean that I've got to walk around in peasant boots and sleep on a stove with a workman and his wife.[10]

However, some critics have based a denial of this supposition on the fact that Tolstoi and his disciples approved of "Ward Number Six" and considered it ideologically akin to them. They also point out that Ragin's philosophy in the story is much more intimately linked with Arthur Schopenhauer's, and that thus it was a polemic against him if against anybody.[11]

Another theory adopted by revolutionary intellectuals, including Lenin, was that "Ward Number Six" was a metaphor for Russia as a whole. Parallels were drawn between Nikita and the tsarist police, between Ragin and the state bureaucracy, and between Gromov and the social revolutionaries. However, it is highly debatable that Chekhov intended "Ward Number Six" as a direct attack on the regime.

The story opens with a naturalistic description of the psychiatric ward in which the predominant words are those that indicate decay and imprisonment. Chekhov steers his reader from the surrounding area of the "lodge," with its nail-studded fence, to the inside where barred windows and nailed-down beds reinforce the prison imagery. The heaps of old garbage and filthy discarded rags which litter the entry are further indicative of the thoroughly depressing sub-human conditions under which the patients live.

The first human being introduced is the guard Nikita, who is described as "simple hearted, practical, and dull-witted" (VII, 271). The first two adjectives are seemingly positive, yet the additional attribute "dull-witted" places a sinister connotation on his character. This is confirmed in the following sentence, where it is mentioned that Nikita "showers blows on the face, on the chest, on the back, on whatever comes first, and is convinced that there would be no order in the place if he did not" (VII, 272).

There are five patients under Nikita's supervision. Gromov is introduced as occupying the third and center bed of the ward, which is indicative of his role in the story in relation to his companions. To his right lie a passive workman with tear-stained eyes and a harmless idiot Jewish shopkeeper; to his left, a nameless autistic glutton and a petty clerk who is suffering from delusions of grandeur. Gromov is the only patient from the upper class, and he is further distinguished from the others by the human quality of his face:

the delicate lines traced on his face by profound, genuine suffering show intelligence and sense, and there is a warm and healthy light in his eyes. I like the man himself, courteous, anxious to be of use, and extraordinarily gentle to everyone except Nikita. When anyone drops a button or a spoon, he jumps up from his bed quickly and picks it up; every day he says good-morning to his companions, and when he goes to bed he wishes them good-night. (VII, 273)

Gromov's background is given in a flashback that draws attention to his dissatisfaction with the meaningless bourgeois life, his wide reading experience, his dogmatism, and his alienation from the others. He had always viewed the townspeople with irritable contempt, declaring that their gross ignorance and torpid animal existence struck him as disgusting. However, gradually this contempt became tinged with fear, and Gromov began to suspect that in this town where any atrocity was possible, he was in personal danger. One morning, when he saw two chained convicts being led through the streets, Gromov could not help but identify himself with their fate. His consequent withdrawal and persecution mania contributed to the actualization of his premonition, and shortly thereafter he was confined to ward six.

Dr. Ragin is first introduced in connection with his eccentric habit of visiting ward six. Such an irregularity warrants explanation, and Dr. Ragin's life history is given as a possible clue to this strange behavior. Although the doctor is heavy and coarse with peasant features, his weak, passive character belies this appearance. Even Ragin's profession as a physician was chosen against his will at the command of his father, and "Andrei Efimych himself had more than once confessed that he had never had a natural bent for medicine" (VII, 279). This is later confirmed by his "indifference" to the substandard hospital he himself directs.

Ignoring injustice and rationalizing the evils around him as inevitable, Ragin escapes into a routine existence of abstract thought and reading. The description of his daily schedule is punctuated by words such as "usually" and "always," while the word "um," meaning intellect, is a characterizing verbal leitmotif. Ragin is constantly preoccupied with "intelligent" books, "intelligent" conversations, and "intelligent" thoughts about the "intellect." However, the fact that Ragin's conscience is not totally anesthetized is indicated at the end of chapter seven when he is unable to sleep after the partial realization of his cowardice:

I serve in a pernicious institution and receive a salary from people whom I am deceiving, I am not honest, but then, I of myself am nothing, I am only part of an inevitable social evil: all local officials are pernicious and receive

their salary for doing nothing . . . And so for my dishonesty it is not I who
am to blame, but the times . . . . (VII, 288)

The initial confrontation between Dr. Ragin and Gromov occurs
quite accidentally. On one of the rare occasions when the doctor is
moved by pity to accept a small amount of responsibility, he decides
to speak to Nikita on behalf of the bare-footed Jew. Yet no sooner
has he made his request than Ragin is met with an abusive tirade
from Gromov:

"The doctor has come!" he shouted, and broke into a laugh. "At
last! Gentlemen, I congratulate you. The doctor is honoring us with a visit.
Cursed reptile!" he shrieked, and stamped in a frenzy such as had never
been seen in the ward before. "Kill the reptile! No, killing's too good.
Drown him in the midden-pit!" (VII, 290)

Ragin's response, "What for?" expresses his genuine feeling of
innocence; because he does not actively contribute to evil, the doctor feels he is absolved from all guilt. A discussion ensues in which
Ragin justifies Gromov's incarceration in ward six as a result of the
laws of probability acting within existing conditions. He goes on to
advise Gromov that "in any surroundings you can find tranquility in
yourself. Free and deep thinking which strives for the comprehension of life, and complete contempt for the foolish bustle of the
world—these are two blessings beyond any that man has ever
known" (VII, 292).

Gromov is understandably enraged. As an individual he is more
than just a victim of probability, and he finds no solace in the
passive example of Diogenes:

"Your Diogenes was a blockhead," said Ivan Dmitrich morosely. "Why do
you talk to me about Diogenes and some foolish comprehension of life?" he
cried, growing suddenly angry and leaping up. "I love life; I love it
passionately. I have the mania of persecution, a continual agonizing terror;
but I have moments when I am overwhelmed by the thirst for life, and then
I am afraid of going mad. I want dreadfully to live, dreadfully!" (VII, 292)

Ragin is delighted to have made the acquaintance of such an
"agreeable young man" and frequently visits Gromov for the
benefit of his conversation. In the discussions that follow all of Dr.
Ragin's references are abstract and philosophical, while Gromov's
arguments remain physical and concrete. What emerges from these

dialogues is that whereas the doctor advocates certain theories about the philosophy of living, Gromov affirms life itself:

"Comprehension . . ." repeated Ivan Dmitrich frowning. "External, internal . . . Excuse me, but I don't understand it. I only know," he said, getting up and looking angrily at the doctor—"I only know that God has created me of warm blood and nerves, yes, indeed! If organic tissue is capable of life it must react to every stimulus. And I do! . . . No sir, it is not philosophy, it's not thinking, it's not breadth of vision, but laziness, fakerism, drowsy stupefaction. Yes," cried Ivan Dmitrich, getting angry again, "you despise suffering, but I'll be bound if you pinch your finger in the door you will howl at the top of your voice." (VII, 295)

And philosophy is not the only point of contrast between Ragin and Gromov. They are also divergent in their personal mannerisms and in their emotional adjustment to life. As opposed to Gromov who was always sickly, Dr. Ragin is physically powerful, "but his step is soft, and his walk is cautious and insinuating." On the other hand, Gromov is "always excited, agitated" and "in the evenings he begins walking rapidly from corner to corner between the bedsteads." Other points of contrast are their voices—Gromov's is a loud tenor, whereas Ragin's is a high soft tenor; their enjoyment of reading—Gromov would "sit nervously pulling at his beard and looking through the magazines and books . . . devouring the pages without giving himself time to digest what he read" (VII, 275), whereas Ragin read "slowly and with concentration, often pausing over a passage which he liked or did not find intelligible" (VII, 283); and their self-assertiveness—Gromov is belligerent in his protestations, while Ragin passively accepts even those things he strongly disapproves of.

Gromov and Ragin are united in that they both perceive the horror and suffering of life. Gromov continues to protest it even in his insanity, whereas Ragin calmly rationalizes pain away with stoic philosophy. Of the two it is Gromov who retains a higher human dignity, and as Ragin gradually perceives this, his identification shifts toward that of his patient.

Chapters 12 through 19 are a dramatization of Ragin's spiritual readjustment, as well as of his transformation in the eyes of society. The first indication of his changed position is the psychiatric examination Ragin is subjected to, after which he broods: " 'My God, they have not a conception of mental pathology!' And for the first time in his life he felt insulted and moved to anger" (VII, 301).

Ragin reacts with his usual indifference when he is dismissed from his job, but his lassitude gradually disappears as the money he had saved becomes depleted. The doctor is no longer shielded from the world by his sacred routine, and it is not so easy for him to ignore injustices that directly concern himself. Ragin's reactions start to mimic those he had earlier observed in Gromov: he often lies silently with his back to his irritating "friend" Mikhail, and finally explodes one day at him screeching, "Go to the devil!" (VII, 309). This is the very expression with which Gromov had dismissed Ragin on his preceding two visits.

The identification between Gromov and Ragin draws closer when the doctor is thrown into ward six and declared insane. Still, even then Ragin makes a gallant attempt to apply his philosophical stoicism, and to summon his indifference as a defense against reality: "Andrei Efimych was even now convinced that there was no difference between his landlady's house and Ward No. 6, that everything in the world was nonsense and vanity of vanities" (VII, 311).

And yet, "In the meanwhile his hands were trembling, his feet were cold, he was filled with dread" (VII, 311). The *fear* that seizes Ragin becomes a leitmotif in chapter 17 which draws attention to his final identity as a victim. Ragin is no longer capable of indifference: the moon, the fence, and the prison are frightening, and Nikita's beating in response to Ragin's anger is still more frightening.

Ragin's epiphany has come too late for anyone, including himself, to benefit from it. He allows himself the final luxury of passively submitting to death, yet without the comfort of immortality that Tolstoi's Ivan Ilich experienced. Ragin's last visions are elusive, but contain beauty and the promise of human communication. His tragedy is that he couldn't perceive in life what was so clear to him in death:

A herd of deer, extraordinarily beautiful and graceful, of which he had been reading the day before, ran by him; then a peasant woman stretched out her hand to him with a registered letter . . . . (VII, 316)

V "The Black Monk" 1894

"The Black Monk" deals with the condition of insanity from a different perspective than that which was employed in "Ward

Number Six." The story's protagonist Kovrin suffers from an over-developed imagination, yet unlike Gromov in "Ward Number Six," his delusions are not paranoic but rather megalomaniac. Kovrin's isolation and retreat from banal pursuits results from an overestimation of his genius, which ultimately leads him to victimize those around him and to destroy himself. Whereas in "Ward Number Six" Chekhov criticized the indifferent brutality of middle class life, this story exposes the danger of the opposite extreme that culminates in Nietzchean madness.

Kovrin's exceptional intelligence and analytic abilities are praised from the beginning of the story by his foster-parent Pesotsky, whose daughter Tanya says:

You were surprised that we had so many of your photographs. But surely you know how my father adores you, worships you. You are a scholar, and not an ordinary man; you have built up a brilliant career, and he is firmly convinced that you turned out a success because he educated you. I do not interfere with his delusion. Let him believe it! (VIII, 82)

Kovrin's refinement thus inspires respect in Pesotsky, who would be a mediocre man were it not for his dedication to maintaining a beautiful garden. Pesotsky's house Borisovka is "large, . . . a-dorned with figures of lions with the plaster falling off" (VII, 80), and he is physically "tall, broad-shouldered and fat." The description of his garden forms the only redemptive aesthetic contrast to Pesotsky's otherwise ugly life:

But the gardens and orchards, which together with the seed-plots occupied some eighty acres, inspired very different feelings. Even in the worst of weather they were bright and joy-inspiring. Such wonderful roses, lilies, camellias, such tulips, such a host of flowering plants of every possible kind and color, from staring white to sooty black—such a wealth of blossoms Kovrin had never seen before. (VIII, 80 - 81)

The word "garden" will later become a verbal leitmotif which underlines Pesotsky's obsession throughout the story with preserving his garden at all costs, and his fear that after his death it will fall to ruin.

On the other hand, Kovrin is a "singularly handsome man" (VIII, 96) who "read much, wrote much, studied Italian . . ." (VIII, 84). He is not disposed to channel all of his energies into the practical application of one idea, but rather responds to beauty through the dilettante appreciation of diverse subjects. His imagination is sensitive to any lyrical note: to childhood memories, to morning dew on the garden roses, to his work, and to music. It is significant that immediately before Kovrin's first hallucination of the black monk he has been listening to a melodious serenade, the words of which describe a "girl with a disordered imagination, who heard by night in a garden some mysterious sounds, sounds so beautiful and strange that she was forced to recognize their harmony and holiness which to us mortals are incomprehensible, and therefore flew back to heaven!" (VIII, 85).

This melody, repeated throughout the story, is heard immediately before Kovrin's perception of the black monk. The second time he appears the monk speaks to Kovrin, informing him that "You serve eternal truth. Your thoughts, your intentions, your astounding science, all your life bears the stamp of divinity, a heavenly impress; . . . the healthy and the normal are but ordinary men—the herd. Fear as to a nervous age, overexhaustion and degeneration can trouble seriously only those whose aims in life lie in the present—that is the herd" (VIII, 91 - 92).

Kovrin fancies that his divine calling as the "bearer of truth" somehow links him to the intensity of Egor Semenovich and Tanya, whose garden is also a sort of "mission." However, Kovrin's marriage to Tanya ironically destroys not only the garden, but also Kovrin's delusions of grandeur. Their unhappy relationship ends after a year, and shortly thereafter Kovrin receives a bitter letter from Tanya that confirms Egor Semenovich's dreaded premonitions concerning his garden:

My father has just died. For this I am indebted to you, for it was you who killed him. Our garden is being ruined; it is managed by strangers; that which my poor father so dreaded is taking place. For this also I am indebted to you. I hate you with all my soul, and wish that you may perish soon! Ah, how I suffer! My heart burns with an intolerable pain! . . . May you be accursed! I took you for an exceptional man, for a genius, I loved you, and you proved a madman . . . . (VIII, 104)

After this letter Kovrin suffers an epiphany which is tragically reminiscent of Dr. Ragin's self-knowledge immediately before death:

His concept led him to speculation on the vanity of the world. He thought of the great price that life demands for the most trivial and ordinary

benefits it gives to men. To reach a chair of professor; to expound com-
monplace thoughts—and those thoughts the thoughts of others—in feeble,
tiresome, heavy language; in one word, to attain the position of a learned
mediocrity, he had studied fifteen years, worked day and night, passed
through a severe psychical disease, survived an unsuccessful marriage—-
been guilty of many follies and injustices which it was torture to remember.
Kovrin now clearly realized that he was a mediocrity, and he was willingly
reconciled to it, for he knew that every man must be satisfied with what he
is . . . . Again he was overtaken by restlessness akin to terror, and it
seemed to him that in the whole hotel except himself there was not one
living soul. (VIII, 105)

Unlike Ragin, Kovrin does not die stripped of his illusions. The
recurrence of the serenade and the appearance of the black monk
inspire in him a renewed faith in his own mystical powers. Kovrin's
impending death does not disillusion him, but rather only confirms
his belief that he is "a genius, and died only because his feeble,
mortal body had lost its balance, and could no longer serve as the
covering of genius" (VIII, 106). When Kovrin's corpse is later discovered by his mistress, "on his face was frozen an immovable smile
of happiness" (VIII, 106). Perhaps Kovrin died in ecstasy, but the
terrible price his delusions exacted from life was not justified.

VI "My Life" 1896

"My Life" continues the pattern of philosophical inquiry that
was begun in "A Boring Story." In this work Chekhov attempts to
define man's position in society with an examination and refutation
of Tolstoi's philosophy of simplification as well as of petty bourgeois
values. His conclusion is that the most basic conflict is not between
"simplicity" and "middle class values" but rather between banality
and beauty.

The theme is first developed with an examination of Misail
Poloznev's rebellion against his father's mediocre values and
brutality. Aleksandr Pavlovich's first words are a rebuke to his son:
"If my dear wife and your mother were living, your life would have
been a source of continual distress to her" (IX, 20). The words
"your life" are purposely used as an ironic contrast to the title "My
Life," and draw attention to the fact that Misail is actually not in
control of his own life. This is confirmed in the subsequent interview between father and son, where Misail passively submits to a
beating:

When my father beat me as a child I had to stand up straight, with my hands held stiffly to my trouser seams, and look him straight in the face. And now when he hit me I was utterly overwhelmed, and, *as though I were still a child*, drew myself up and tried to look him in the face. (IX, 22)

Misail's failure to develop a responsible, adult identity is further revealed in his poor marks at school, his inability to strive for a job that might interest him, his sloppy attire, and his position working offstage in the town's amateur plays. However, Misail justifies his decision to become a laborer on moral grounds, rather than recognizing his own weaknesses:

I expressed this idea: that what is wanted is that the strong should not enslave the weak, that the minority should not be a parasite on the majority, not a vampire forever sucking its vital sap: that is, all, without exception, strong and weak, rich and poor, should take part equally in the struggle for existence . . . and there is no better means for equalizing things in that way than manual labor, in the form of universal service, compulsory for all. (IX, 43)

Misail's acquaintance, Dr. Blagovo, disagrees with this conception, and voices a protest that expresses Chekhov's own doubts as to its validity:

. . . don't you consider that if you had spent your strength of will, this strained activity, all these powers on something else, for instance, on gradually becoming a great scientist or artist, your life would have been broader and deeper and would have been more productive? . . . And don't you think that if everyone, including the best men, the thinkers and great scientists, taking part in the struggle for existence, each on his own account, is going to waste his time breaking stones and painting roofs, may not that threaten a grave danger to progress? (IX, 42 - 43)

Misail's defense, that it is more important to "fulfill the moral law" (IX, 43) sounds weak and infantile before Dr. Blagovo's impassioned faith in the aspiring future of mankind.

Misail's values are challenged again in his marriage to the beautiful and talented Mariya Dolzikova. Mariya is a cultured rich girl who has studied opera, and who falls in love with Misail in conjunction with a temporary allegiance to Tolstoian values. However, Mariya is not nearly so enamored of "the simple life" as it is in reality, and leaves her husband because she realizes:

Other methods of struggle are needed, strong, bold, rapid ones . . . . If one really wants to be of use, one must get out of the narrow circle of ordinary activity and try to act directly . . . Why is it that art, and music, for example, is so living, so popular and in reality so powerful? Because the musician or singer affects thousands at once . . . Dear, dear art. Art gives wings . . . Anyone who is tired . . . of petty interests can find peace and satisfaction only in the *beautiful.* (IX, 75 - 76).

The fault with Misail's philosophy is that it would never lead a man to accomplish something great or beautiful, and almost inevitably it entails more compromises with "middle class" values than expected. Although Misail's critique of his father and their neighbors is well founded, his life accomplishes nothing toward remedying that situation. His nickname "little-use" is thus well chosen: an innocuous and contributing member of society, Misail nevertheless remains a slave to those people he had thought to rebel against in becoming a laborer. Chekhov thus cogently refutes Tolstoi's doctrine of simplicity with the example of Misail's life. His character's proud words at the end of the story reveal the pathetic impotence of Misail's actual accomplishments:

What I have been through has not been for nothing. My great troubles, my patience, have touched people's hearts, and now they don't call me "Better-than nothing," they don't laugh at me, and when I walk by the shops they don't throw water over me . . . . people are glad to give me orders, and I am now considered a first-rate workman, and the best foreman after Radish . . . People are civil to me, they address me politely, and in the houses where I work they offer me tea and send to inquire whether I wouldn't like dinner. Children and young girls often come and look at me with curiosity and compassion. (IX, 92 - 93)

"Ward Number Six" and "The Black Monk" offer vivid portraits of insanity. But this is a topic uncharacteristic of the developing Chekhov, most of whose last stories are concerned with ordinary people and the adjustments to life with which they attempt to create meaning. Chekhov explores the themes of death and of love, of the compromises one makes in life by exchanging youthful ideals for a comfortable routine, and he questions whether the ideals or noble aspirations are not as illusory and prosaic as the life they attempt to defy.

CHAPTER 5

Search for Love and Home

W HEN Chekhov wrote to Suvorin that he needed to live among people away from the city, he was expressing a longing for a place where he could feel at home and where, at the same time, he would be free to wander in the country and have the tranquility and the solace of nature to help him create his imaginary world. But at the same time, he was also expressing a longing for a place of his own, a place where he could not only retreat to work, but which would satisfy his desire for family, stability, and possession.

It was at the time he wrote that letter to Suvorin (Oct. 19, 1891) that he began to look for a country house, and was trying even to buy a small farm in the Ukraine. So impatient was he to become a home owner that he agreed to buy Melikhovo, an estate that his sister and brother found, without seeing it. And once they moved to the estate, Chekhov gave way to his passion for tree-planting. He also planted a lot of flowers, stocked the ponds with fish, acquired horses, a cow and two dogs, "Bromide" and "Quinine."

Chekhov, it seems, wanted to reinstate the family life he once knew in Taganrog, only with himself as its head and without the father's tyranny, in more idealized circumstances. Indeed his father became the choirmaster in the local church at Melikhovo and Chekhov became a member of the Sanitary Council in the country. The villagers came to him to be healed and the editors of the new medical journal, *The Surgical Chronicle*, asked Chekhov's help when the journal was about to fail. Soon Chekhov was involved with the local government, with building a new road to the railroad station, and with building new schools. In short, "Father Antosha's" responsibilities expanded beyond his immediate family into the community of Melikhovo where he found a new home. And as he accepted the role of the village patriarch, where he lived among people, with his family, and was constantly visited by Moscow friends, his thoughts must have turned to personal happiness. "As I watch spring," he wrote to Suvorin on March 17, 1892, "I am terribly eager for a paradise in the Beyond. In a word, there are moments when I am so happy that I susperstitiously pull myself up and remember my creditors. . . ."[1] This sense of happiness continued and at the end of summer he wrote to Suvorin, "I liked life and wanted to live. How many trees I planted!" (Oct. 10, 1892).[2]

The desire to beautify his estate was not the only motivation behind his passion for tree-planting, there must have been also the desire to endure, the need to leave something living after one's death. His later request to his wife, Olga, to give him a son, was surely not a sudden change, but more likely an old dream which then found a legitimate expression. And yet he could not find the kind of woman who would inspire in him a strong emotion and a sense of commitment. And to his mother's and friends' admonitions to get married, Chekhov always replied in a bantering tone that he wanted a wife who would change nothing in his life, who would be, "like the moon, and won't appear in my life every day."

Only after repeated goading from his brother, Misha, did Chekhov reply seriously concerning his thoughts on marriage:

As for marriage, on which you insist—what can I say? There's no use marrying except for love; to marry a girl simply because she is likable is comparable to buying yourself something at the market simply because it is all right. The most important nut in married life is love, sexual attraction, one flesh; all the rest is unreliable and dull, no matter how wisely we calculate.[3] (Oct. 26, 1898)

Nemrovich - Danchenko in his memoirs writes that although Chekhov was very appealing to women and had some love affairs, his attachments did not last too long. He adds that Chekhov never gossiped on this subject and before his marriage to Olga Knipper was probably never in love. Indeed, the only love letters in his correspondence are those to Olga Knipper. Nevertheless, the ideas of love and marriage and family love must have occupied his mind when he lived at Melikhovo for these are the themes that begin to predominate his writing starting in 1894. He certainly knew all along how vital love, or dreams of love, are in man's psychological makeup, that it is the only emotion that gives meaning to the vast indifference of life. Yet, as with everything else, Chekhov knew better than to sentimentalize love or family life; he knew that the prose of life can destroy the romantic aspect of any relationship. He also knew that for him, as for any artist, even the very best family life, love and the comforts of home, could be disabling. It was not the torpor of Oblomovism that he was afraid of, but the satisfactions brought to a man by an amiable wife, by pleasing surroundings, and by the flowers, trees, and berries planted in a homage to beauty and for aesthetic contemplation. Such satisfaction often results in creative inertia.

Chekhov's fears were not precisely defined. He was afraid of the inability to love in both the primitive men like Bronza in his *Rothschild's Fiddle*, or in the more educated men like Laptev in *Three Years*. He was afraid of the pragmatism that destroys the dreamlike love of Misyus and the artist in the *House with the Mezzanine*, of what the passage of time does to any expression of youthful idealism. But most of all he was afraid of life in a shell, the life that, whether by choice or circumstances, imprisons the spirit or renders it impotent, either by easy comforts or by providing any kind of escape from the complexities of life. Aware as he was of the multitude of complexities, Chekhov nevertheless consistently refused any obvious solutions. He approached every question that preoccupied him not with the idea of solving it, but with the desire to discover as many aspects of it as possible and to examine the variety of potential solutions.

It is fitting that the last two stories Chekhov wrote, "The Bishop" and "The Bride," should have such tentative endings. In "The Bishop," added to the grief of a man realizing that his life is about to end, is the gentle lament of one for whom fame and importance are no substitute for a more simple communion with those he loves. In place of his glorified position the bishop would have preferred the simple faith of his childhood and his mother's caresses. But in "The Bride," Nadya, the heroine, leaves her home and family for what she believes will be ". . .vast, infinitely spacious life." Chekhov desired both—the solace of home and the mysteries of the unknown. He was also aware of the perils and the joys of both tranquility and exploration. He refused neither in his life and in his work.

I   "Rothschild's Fiddle"

"Rothschild's Fiddle" (1894) describes the emotional poverty of the coffin-maker, Bronza, who can only define his life in terms of the losses he sustains. There is little joy or pleasure in Bronza's preoccupation with his financial deficit, yet he is firmly entrenched in the pattern of interpreting everything within this framework. As the title indicates, his violin and all the potentialities it embodies will ultimately assume a greater value to Bronza.

His wife's illness and subsequent death have the initial effect of temporarily shifting the coffin-maker's attention from his financial losses to his spiritual impotence. It's clear from her joy and eagerness to die that Marfa welcomes any sort of liberation from life with her husband. Bronza recalls that

All his life he had never treated her kindly, never caressed her, never pitied her, never thought of buying her a kerchief for her head . . . but only roared at her, abused her for her losses, and rushed at her with shut fists . . . and now, beginning to understand why she had such a strange, enraptured face, he felt uncomfortable. (VIII, 142)

Another indication of Bronza's and Marfa's bleak life together is the old woman's lyrical recollection of their small, blond-haired daughter who died fifty years earlier. Bronza doesn't even remember his wife's description of the happy moments they spent together singing under the willows; rather he is preoccupied with the loss of the two rubles, forty kopecks which Marfa's coffin cost him.

It is only later, after Marfa has been buried with satisfying "honour, order and cheapness" (VIII, 144), that Bronza sits under the willow tree his wife had mentioned, and for the first time notices the loveliness of the river flowing by. At first he reckons its beauty in terms of profit and losses, estimating the river's possibilities for accruing wealth, but gradually the word "loss" is transferred to an aesthetic, spiritual level:

But look backward—nothing but losses, such losses that to think of them makes the blood run cold. And why cannot a man live without these losses? Why had the birch wood and the pine forest both been cut down? Why is the common pasture unused? Why do people do exactly what they ought not to do? Why did he all his life scream, roar, clench his fists, insult his wife? For what imaginable purpose did he frighten and insult the Jew? Why, indeed, do people prevent one another from living in peace? All these are also losses! Terrible losses! If it were not for hatred and malice people would draw from one another incalculable profits. (VIII, 146)

The following day Bronza is ill and knows that he will soon die.

At this point the word "profit" ironically replaces "loss" as the verbal leitmotif: Bronza muses

that from death at least there would be one profit; it would no longer be necessary to eat, to drink, to pay taxes, or to injure others; and as a man lies in his grave not one year, but hundreds and thousands of years, the profit was enormous. The life of man was, in short, a loss, and only his death a profit. (VIII, 146)

Bronza thus does not regret the passing of his life, but rather life itself. He is filled with sorrow that everything beautiful in the world must decay, including his fiddle, the birch wood, and the pine forest, and in one of his few generous moments plays the fiddle with compassion for this life "full of losses." Bronza's redemption becomes complete when in a burst of good feeling, he wills the beloved fiddle to his former enemy, the Jew Rothschild.

But the story ends on an ironic note. After Bronza's death Rothschild has learned to imitate his sad melody that was inspired by pity for life's decay, and has turned it into an economic "gain." The last sentence draws attention to the materialistic pettiness that permeates life and which makes people deaf to its real meaning:

But this new song so pleases everyone in the town that wealthy traders and officials never fail to engage Rothschild for their social gatherings, and even force him to play it as many as ten times. (VIII, 147)

II "The House with the Mezzanine"

"The House with the Mezzanine" (1896) was greeted as both a lyrical love story and as a political polemic. The most liberal newspaper of the time, *Russkie vedomosti*, commented that the artist-hero of the story was a "typical representative of the 'gloomy people' . . . whose traits are boredom, absence of inspiration, knowledge of their inability to carry on everyday business and absence of social instinct."[4] Another liberal newspaper, *Birzhevye vedomosti*, confirmed this opinion, stating that the artist was a negative character in contrast to Lida, who embodied "young strength and dedication to service."[5]

Indeed, the contrast between the artist's lackadaisical, lyrical nature and Lida's pragmatic self-assertiveness is developed from their first meeting. Lida's physical description, "beautiful with a

small stubborn mouth and a stern expression" (IX, 6), is indicative
of her dogmatic, judgmental reaction to life. Throughout the story
her harsh personality is depicted by the tone and content of her
dialogue: "She spoke much and loudly, a habit perhaps acquired as
a teacher" (IX, 8); "Grave and unsmiling, she asked him why he did
not work in the zemstvo (county council)" (IX, 7), " 'It's not right
. . .' she said reproachfully, 'it's a shame' " (IX, 7); "Whenever a
serious discussion got under way she would say to me coldly, 'This
won't interest you' " (IX, 13).

In contrast to this, the artist's adjustment to life is summed up by
himself in the following words, "Condemned by destiny to
perpetual idleness, I did absolutely nothing" (IX, 5). He also has little faith in the value of his work, admitting that "From my earliest
days I've been wrung by envy, self-dissatisfaction, and distrust in
my work" (IX, 12).

It is highly doubtful that Chekhov intended to elevate Lida's
worth above that of the artist in this story. Nor would it seem that
Lida's political role is negative, while the artist is a socialist
visionary, as Soviet critics suggest.[6] The ideological conflict
between these two characters is stated with Chekhov's usual objectivity, and his own position in relation to it is ambiguous.

The lyrical love that develops between the narrator and Lida's
younger sister Misyus forms the artistic core of the story. Misyus's
large naive eyes, her passive idealism, and her naiveté appeal
strongly to the artist and draw him to her. The subjective description of his love for Misyus is developed by the narrator in conjunction with his impressions of nature: When he first sees the house
with the mezzannine, the artist forms a magical yet melancholy impression that foreshadows his doomed relationship with Misyus:

Once on my way home I happened upon an estate I had never seen before.
The sun was already setting, and the evening shadows lay over the ripening
rye. There were two rows of ancient towering fir trees, planted so close
together that they formed two parallel walls enclosing an avenue of somber
beauty. It was quiet and dark but for the occasional gleams of golden light
shimmering high in the treetops, painting the spiders' webs in rainbow
colors. Suffocating and overpowering was the fragrance of the pines. I soon
turned into a long avenue of lime trees. Here, too, everything spoke of
neglect and age. Last year's leaves rustled mornfully beneath my feet, and
shadows lurked in the twilight between the trees. . . . I went past a white
house with a terrace and a mezzanine, and quite suddenly there unfolded
before my eyes a view of the manorial courtyard . . . For a moment I was

under the spell of something very dear and familiar to me: it was as though I had seen this . . . in the days of my childhood. (IX, 5 - 6)

Whereas descriptions of Lida almost invariably are set inside the house, the artist pictures Misyus in natural settings that enhance her beauty. Misyus reads on "the terrace, . . . in a deep armchair, her feet scarcely touching the ground, or she would hide away with the book somewhere in the avenue of lime trees, or she would pass through the gate into the open fields" (IX, 9). The artist recalls days they spent together boating, or gathering cherries, and mentions that "her thin, delicate arms gleamed through her wide sleeves" (IX, 9).

Nature descriptions are also used to foreshadow the threat that Lida poses to the artist's and Misyus's relationship. Misyus's awe before both the artist and her sister reveals her divided loyalties:

Zhenya [Misyus] supposed that because I was a painter I must know a good deal and could accurately divine anything I did not know. She longed for me to lead her into the realm of the eternal and the beautiful, into that higher world where she thought I was at home, and she talked to me about God, about Life everlasting, and about the miraculous. And I, who refuse to believe that I and my imagination will perish . . . would reply "Yes. People are immortal". . . . We were going home when she suddenly paused and said, "Our Lida is a remarkable person, isn't she—I adore her passionately and would lay down my life for her at any moment. Tell me"—Zhenya touched my sleeve with her finger—"tell me why are you always fighting with her? Why do you get so irritated?" (IX, 10)

Later in the afternoon after this conversation "The whole sky was overcast, and a fine thin rain began to fall . . . Now as the rain fell softly we spoke about Lida, 'Yes, she is a remarkable person' her mother said" (IX, 11).

In the end Lida's decisive, aggressive decision to terminate the artist's relationship with her sister succeeds, and Misyus is sent away from the town. The night before Misyus leaves, when she and the artist confess their love for each other, the nature description again foreshadows the tragic denouncement of their friendship:

It was a melancholy August night—melancholy because there was already a breath of autumn in the air. The moon was rising behind a purple cloud, shedding scarcely any light along the road and the dark fields of winter wheat stretching away on both sides. At times a shooting star would fall.

Zhenya walked beside me, and she avoided looking up at the sky so as not to see the falling stars, which for some reason frightened her. (IX, 17)

The fact that both Misyus and the artist bow to Lida's decree underlies the dreamlike passivity of their love. Yet the purity and beauty of their feelings remain unscathed. The narrator's last line: "Misyus, where are you?" (IX, 19) is an evocation of the eternal love the artist will always feel for Misyus, which transcends the temporal domination Lida attained.

III "The Peasants" 1897

When "The Peasants" was published in 1897, it immediately produced a polemic between the legal Marxist P. B. Struve and the narodnik (Populist) liberal N. K. Mikhailovsky. Struve argued that Chekhov correctly portrayed the idiocy of village life as opposed to the advantages of city civilization, whereas Mikhailovsky flatly stated that the story was biased.[7] Chekhov's "The Peasants" is not so much a naturalistic social commentary on rural life as it is an exposé of the dehumanizing effects of poverty everywhere.

Chekhov defines Nikolai Chikildeev in the opening sentence with the word *lakei* (servant). The remaining information in the first paragraph robs Nikolai of this identity, explaining that he has become too old and ill to hold a job. With no active present and no future to look forward to, the old man seeks refuge in his past. He still retains fond memories of his peasant village, and soothing himself with the folk saying "there is help in the walls of home" (IX, 95), he decides to return there with his wife Olga and daughter Sasha.

Nikolai realizes his mistake with his first glance at the cabin he had remembered as being "bright, cozy, and comfortable" (IX, 95). It is now "dark, crowded, and squalid" (IX, 95). A filthy, lopsided stove occupies an entire half of the room, scraps of old newspaper decorate the walls, and to make matters worse, there are flies swarming everywhere. Nikolai's niece, a flaxen-haired girl of eight, is sitting apathetically on the stove, and does not even bother to introduce herself. A cat rubbing itself against an oven fork also fails to respond to Sasha's greeting "Pussy, Pussy!" The girl's indifferent explanation for the animal's uncommunicativeness elucidates the psychological reason for her own silence: "It can't hear. It was hit" (IX, 95).

The two other squalid cabins in the small village are only slightly better than the Chikildeev's, but the "willows, elders and mountain ash peeping out from the courtyards had a pleasant look" (IX, 95). Indeed, the beauty of nature presents a pleasing contrast to these unsightly dwellings:

Sitting on the edge of the ravine, Nikolai and Olga watched the sunset, and saw how the gold and crimson sky was reflected in the river, in the church windows, and in the very air, which was soft and still and inexpressibly pure, as it never was in Moscow. And when the sun had set, . . . geese flew across from the other side of the river, and then all was hushed; the soft light faded from the air, and dusk began its rapid descent. (IX, 96)

"With the descent of dusk" the Chikildeev family returns home from work, reintroducing the themes of poverty and ugliness into the narrative. Chekhov purposely does not give individual portraits of these people. Rather they are depicted with the use of synecdotal details that stress the lack of choice and identity in their lives: Nikolai's parents are "bent and toothless" (IX, 96); his two sisters-in-law are "strong and broad-shouldered" (IX, 96); his brother "growls like a beast . . . but is no breadwinner"; and his eight-year-old niece is silently apathetic.

There is no genuine love between the members of this family, who live according to their lowest possible potentials as human beings. The routine religiosity that substitutes for real emotion in their relationships is sadly ironical. The entire family ignores Marya's pleas to spare her Kiryak's violent beating, and it is only after she has been duly punched in the face that Kiryak's father mutters, "Before guests too! What a sin!" (IX, 97). The religious irony increases when in an attempt to restore his image before "guests," Kiryak prays in front of an icon. He has offered no apology to his wife, and clearly he feels no real regret for his action. Examples of this sort of ersatz religiosity appear throughout the narrative: Kiryak complains to Christ of the evil effects of vodka on him, but refuses to remain sober for even a day, Olga can only repeat "Oh holy saints" in response to the brutal behavior around her, and the irritable granny, who wrathfully whips her granddaughters for minor offenses, screams "Christians, all you who believe in God! Darlings, they're trampling on me! Oh, oh darlings, come and save me!" (IX, 113) when she is threatened with the loss of her samovar!

The ignorance and utter torpor of the peasants are also satirized. In chapter 5, a fire threatens to destroy the village, but all the men are drunk, the few hard-working women tire, and the others prefer to trust in the power of their icons. The village headman screams "Pump! Lend a hand, good Orthodox folk," but "the peasants stood around in a crowd doing nothing and staring at the fire" (IX, 197). It is only with the aid of some educated gentry from across the river that the fire is finally put out, and their efficiency is a further mockery of the peasant's inability to control his condition.

The peasants' utter resigned hopelessness is also underlined in their attitude toward death;

Only the well-to-do peasants were afraid of death: the richer they grew the less they believed in God and in the salvation of the soul, and only through fear of their earthly end did they light candles and have Masses said, in order to be on the safe side. The poorer peasants did not fear death. The old man and Granny were told to their faces that they had lived too long, that it was time they were dead, and they did not mind. They did not scruple to tell Feokla in Nikolai's presence that when Nikolai died her husband Denis would be discharged from the army . . . And Marya, far from dreading death, regretted that it was so long in coming, and was glad when her children died. (IX, 17)

The story ends on a pessimistic note. Nikolai dies after an ignorant healer prescribes a massive "blood letting cure" that would probably also have killed a healthy man half his age. His wife Olga and daughter Sasha are no longer welcome in the cabin and must wander from village to village seeking alms. Yet despite all the indifference and brutality she had witnessed, Olga feels regret at leaving the peasant village. Her feelings perhaps reflect Chekhov's own understanding of the situation:

During the summer and the winter there had been hours and days when it seemed as though these people lived worse than cattle, and it was terrible to be with them; they were coarse, dishonest, dirty, and drunken; they did not live at peace with one another but quarreled continually, because they feared, suspected, and despised each other. Who keeps the tavern and encourages drunkenness? The peasant. Who embezzles, and drinks up the funds that belong to the community, the schools, the church? The peasant. Who steals from his neighbors, sets fire to their property, bears false witness to a court for a bottle of vodka? . . . Yes, to live with them was terrible; but yet, they were human beings, they suffered and wept like human beings, and there was nothing in their lives for which one could not find justification. Crushing labor that made the whole body ache at night, cruel winters, scanty crops, overcrowding, and no help, and nowhere to look for help . . . And indeed, can any sort of help or good example be given by the lazy, grasping, greedy, dissolute men who only visit the village in order to outrage, to despoil, to terrorize? Olga recalled the wretched, humiliated look of the old folks when in the winter Kiryak had been led off to be flogged . . . And now she felt sorry for all these people, it hurt her, and as she walked on she kept looking back at the cabins. (IX, 119)

IV "The Native Corner" *1897*

"The Native Corner" (1897) further develops the themes of imagination versus reality dealt with in "The Steppe." In this story the heroine is a twenty-three-year-old orphan who is traveling to her aunt's home on the steppe. The opening few paragraphs reveal both the loneliness and the sense of optimism that Vera feels as she embarks on her journey:

It is on the Donets railway. The mournful white station stands in solitude in the steppe. It is quiet, the walls are heated by the blazing sun, and there is no shade at all and, so it seems, no people about. The train has already pulled out, leaving you there. It was a thirty verst distance from the station, and Vera, too, could not resist the charm of the steppe, forgot about the past and thought only how much space and freedom there were here, this space and freedom were what she—healthy, intelligent, beautiful, and young—had been missing all her life. (IX, 129)

Upon her arrival home Vera is filled with joy at the warm welcome showered on her by Aunt Dasha and her grandfather, and she is soothed by a soft, comfortable bed, but this blissful impression is modified the next morning when Vera inspects her home more closely. The garden is "old, ugly and neglected" (IX, 131). Unwilling to entertain a negative opinion about her aunt's house, Vera attempts to calm any misgivings by again speculating on the wide and beautiful expanse of the steppe.

Unfortunately, every incident from this point on serves to narrow further the possibilities of Vera's life, until she realizes she is indeed living in "a corner" as the title suggests. The highly praised and "eligible" bachelor Dr. Neshchapov is described as a silent "mediocrity," whose unctuous manners hardly recommend him. Vera is also indignant at her aunt's despotic disposition, which makes life miserable for the servants in the house:

There was always a feeling of torment whenever the aunt made jam with a very serious face, as though she were performing a religious rite, the short sleeves exposing her small despotic hands and the servants running back and forth, bustling round the jam they would never eat. (IX, 136)

Vera's grandfather is senile and gluttonish, offering little solace to her, and thus Vera feels totally isolated and unable to control her situation:

She was vexed and hated her aunt. Her aunt made her sick, filling her with loathing. But what was she to do? Cut her short? Be rude to her? But what would be the use of that? Supposing she should resist her, remove her and render her harmless, and force the grandfather to stop brandishing his stick, what purpose would that serve? It would be the same as killing one mouse or one snake in the boundless steppe. The huge expanses, the long winters, the monotony and boredom instilled a sense of helplessness, made the situation look hopeless, and you did not feel like doing anything because it was of no use anyway. (IX, 137)

The indifference of the steppe has communicated itself to the human beings living there, whereas all the beauty and freedom of its wide open space is ignored. At the end of "The Native Corner," Vera has degenerated to the same level as her aunt: she begins to abuse the servants and no longer even asks herself "What am I to do?" As an antidote to the emptiness of her life Vera decides to marry Dr. Neshohapov, whom she scorns, yet she is finally convinced that compromise is necessary.

Beautiful nature, dreams and music speak of something that is far removed from reality. Happiness and truth evidently exist somewhere outside life. One must not live but merge with this magnificent steppe, which with is flowers, hills and distances is as endless and indifferent as eternity, and then everything will be all right. (IX, 138)

CHAPTER 6

Search for Escapes

I "The Man in a Shell" 1898

IN 1898 three stories that would later be considered a
trilogy were published in *Russian Thought*. "The Man in a
Shell," "Gooseberries," and "About Love" are united by their con-
tinuity of characterization, as well as by their common thematic
structure. In these stories three men listen to one another's personal
anecdotes: the high school teacher Burkin, the veterinary surgeon
Ivan Ivanych, and the landowner Alekhin; each relates an experience illustrative of *futliarnost'* (an insular existence), revealing
much of themselves as each attempts to guide the others.

"The Man in a Shell" first introduces the theme of *futliarnost'*
with Burkin's and Ivanych's remarks concerning Mavra, an acquaintance who has hardly left her stove for ten years. Both agree
that a withdrawn behavior is hardly unusual, yet they find it difficult to account for the wide prevalence of such a rigid, passive adjustment to life.

Burkin decides to expound on this philosophical problem, offering an interpretive description of the archetypal personification of
futliarnost', his late colleague Belikov. The leitmotif that becomes
associated with this man is his constant apprehension, "You can
never tell what might come of it!" Belikov is afraid of any emotion
or behavior that does not conform to a rigidly set pattern:

. . . Only government regulations and newspaper notices in which
something was prohibited were clear to him. If some ruling forbade that
pupils be outside after nine o'clock at night, or some article prohibited car-
nal love, then this was clear and definite to him: it was forbidden and that
was that! But in any permission or authorization there remained for him
always an element of doubt, something not fully expressed, something
hazy. When a dramatic circle was permitted in town, or a reading room, or

teahouse, he would shake his head and say quietly: 'That is of course all very well, to be sure, all this is very good, but I hope there won't be some consequence.' . . . If one of his colleagues was late for Mass, if there were rumors of some prank played by the students, if a female teacher was seen late at night in the company of an officer, he would be very disturbed and repeat that he hoped there wouldn't be some consequence. (IX, 147)

Yet much more disturbing than Belikov's idiosyncratic attitude was the almost hypnotic power he exerted over the whole town:

Under the influence of people like Belikov the whole town spent ten to fifteen frightened years. We were afraid to speak out loud, to write letters, to make acquaintances, to read books, to help the poor, to teach people how to read and write. (IX, 148)

The Soviet critic Berdnikov interprets Belikov as a symbol of the nineteenth-century Russian government and comments: "The hostility of the existing order to man is powerfully shown in this story."[1] It is clear that Chekhov's emphasis is not on the repressive political structure, but rather on the fact that men can so lightly sacrifice their freedom, becoming slaves at the slightest pretext.

Another interesting interpretation of Belikov's identity is espoused by the novelist Joseph Conrad, who maintains that there are definite parallels between him and Dostoevsky's underground man. There certainly are several obvious similarities between these two characters: both have aged male servants, both feel that they are living in a "corner," and both fall in love. However, there is a reversed relationship of conscious intention to its effect on other people in these two men. Belikov succeeds in enslaving others, although he harbors no theory of man's desire to forfeit his freedom to another consciousness. On the other hand, the underground man understands the reasons for domination of one man by another, but he himself has no influence on anyone but Liza.

The magnetic power that Belikov's slavish mentality exerts on other people can be broken only by a positive life force that refuses to conform. This life force is introduced with the description of the new Ukrainian teacher, Kovalenko, and his sister, Varenka. Both of these characters are depicted with their loud voices, his "which seems to come out of a barrel 'Boom, boom, boom' " (IX, 149) and hers which is either lilting in song or ringing with laughter, and by their robust good health. The townspeople out of sheer boredom tacitly agree that Belikov should marry Varenka and do everything they can to encourage the budding romance between them.

Belikov's attraction to Varenka makes him more human, yet at the same time renders him vulnerable. The caricatured portrait of Belikov with Varenka entitled "Anthropos in Love" and his humiliation after Kovalenko has thrown him down a staircase are unbearable to the teacher. These two incidents are fatal because they force Belikov to acknowledge his own absurdity. He chooses to ensconce himself in the final shell of death rather than adjust to life.

When Burkin has finished with his story he goes outside and looks at the moon. A lyrical passage follows that underlines both men's receptivity to life, and at this point Ivan Ivanych responds with some illuminating comments concerning the story:

Yes, that's the way it is, repeated Ivan Ivanych; and isn't our living in the airless, crowded town, our writing useless papers, our playing vint—isn't all this a sort of shell for us? And this spending our lives among pettifogging idle men and silly, unoccupied women, our talking and our listening to all sorts of poppycock, isn't that a shell, too? If you like, I will tell you a very instructive story. (IX, 156)

Yet at this point, Burkin is ironically impervious to further discussion, as though he no longer wants to explore the subject he himself initiated. Both men return to the dark, protective barn and lie down to sleep. Mavra's footsteps, that are familiar only with the small plot of land she lives on, are heard a moment later, and remind the agitated Ivan Ivanych of the futility of life in a shell:

"To see and hear them lie," said Ivan Ivanych, turning over on the other side, "and to be called a fool for putting up with their lies; to endure insult and humiliation, and not dare say openly that you are on the side of the honest and the free, and to lie and smile yourself, and all for the sake of a crust of bread, . . . no, one cannot go on living like that!" (IX, 156)

Again Burkin pleads that they go to sleep, but Ivan Ivanych feels a need to remain awake. He sits gazing out of doors at the wide expanse of moonlit night, conscious of man's failure to realize his limitless possibilities.

II "Gooseberries"

"Gooseberries" continues the narrative thread begun in "The Man in a Shell." The story opens with a description of Burkin and

Ivan Ivanych walking on the open plain, where the vast landscape appears endless and beautiful to them. There is a mild pensive mood in nature that is somewhat reminiscent of the serene moonlit night the two men spent together in the barn, and perhaps this association leads Burkin to mention the story Ivan had desired to relate that night.

Ivan had intended to talk about his brother, but before he can begin the story it starts to rain. The two men seek refuge at a friend's, Alekhin's, house, where the theme of the beauty of nature is again introduced with Ivan's idyllic swim in the river.

The opening mood created by the wide unfenced expanse of the steppe is deliberately developed as a contrast to Ivan Ivanych's subsequent narration. Ivan speaks of his brother Nikolai Ivanych's obsession with acquiring a country estate, and remarks that he never sympathized with his brother's desire "to shut himself up for the rest of his life on a little property of his own. It is a common saying that a man needs only six feet of earth. But six feet is what a corpse needs, not a man" (IX, 160). Ivan's comment, as many critics have already noted, establishes an association with Tolstoi's didactic story "How Much Land Does Man Need?" in which Tolstoi concludes that man needs only enough earth to be buried in. Both authors agree that greed is destructive to freedom, but whereas Tolstoi's tale refutes ambitious desire altogether, "Gooseberries" attempts to shift its focus from petty, personal goals to wider, more humanistic pursuits:

To retire from the city, from the struggle, from the hubbub, to go off and hide on one's own farm—that's not life, it is selfishness, sloth, it is a kind of monasticism, but monasticism without works. Man needs not six feet of earth, not a farm, but the whole globe, all of Nature, where unhindered he can display all the capacities and peculiarities of his free spirit. (IX, 160)

Ivan's description of Nikolai's life is one of Chekhov's most powerful portraits of the blind and sometimes destructive powers of banal romanticism. Nikolai deprives himself of food, of youthful enjoyment, and of love, and even drives his wife to her death—all because he

dreamed of eating his own *shchi* [sour cabbage soup], which would fill the whole farmyard with a delicious aroma, of picnicking on the green grass, of sleeping in the sun, of sitting for hours on the seat by the gate at field and forest. Books on agriculture and the farming items in almanacs were his joy, the delight of his soul . . . And he pictured to himself garden paths, flowers, fruit, bird houses with starlings in them, crucians in the pond, and all that sort of thing, you know. These imaginary pictures varied . . . but somehow gooseberry bushes figured in every one of them. . . . (IX, 160)

The pathos of Nikolai's sacrifice and cruelty in order to attain his patch of land only increases after his dream has been realized. To begin with, the land itself hardly conforms to the idealized image Nikolai had dreamed about:

Through an agent my brother bought a mortgaged estate of three hundred acres with a house, servant's quarters, a park, but with no orchard, no gooseberry patch, no duck pond. There was a stream, but the water in it was the color of coffee, for on one of its banks there was a brickyard and on the other a glue factory. But my brother was not disconcerted. (IX, 161)

Neither is Nikolai disconcerted when he tastes his first batch of homegrown but sour gooseberries. "He looked at the gooseberries in silence, with tears in his eyes. He could not speak for excitement . . . with the triumph of a child . . . he ate the gooseberries greedily, and kept repeating 'How tasty' " (IX, 162).

Chekhov does not merely describe Nikolai's life in the country with such bathetic undertones. His depiction of that man's slothful yet high-handed morality also contains a vituperative denunciation of liberalism. When Ivan Ivanych first visits the estate, his initial impression centers on the selfish, pretentious life his brother leads there:

I made my way to the house and was met by a fat dog with reddish hair that looked like a pig. It wanted to bark, but was too lazy. The cook, a fat barelegged woman, who also looked like a pig, came out of the kitchen and said that the master was resting after dinner. I . . . found him sitting up in bed. . . . He had grown older, stouter, flabby . . . it looked as though he might grunt at any moment. . . . He was no longer the poor, timid clerk he used to be but a real landowner, a gentleman. . . . And he concerned himself with his soul's welfare too in a substantial, upperclass manner, and performed good deeds not simply, but pompously. He dosed the peasants . . . and then treated the villagers to a gallon of vodka. . . . Nikolai Ivanych, who when he was a petty official was afraid to have opinions of his own even if he kept them to himself, now uttered nothing but incontrovertible truths and did so in the tone of a minister of state: "Education is necessary, but the masses are not ready for it . . . I know the common people, they love me. I only have to raise my little finger, and they will do anything I want." (IX, 161 - 62)

Although Nikolai is happy, Ivan questions his brother's smug contentment that is oblivious to the suffering around him. The theme of *futliarnost'* is thus transferred onto a political level, and Ivan comments:

Look at life: the insolence and idleness of the strong, the ignorance and brutishness of the weak, horrible poverty everywhere, overcrowding, degeneration, drunkenness, hypocrisy, lying . . . but we do not see or hear those who suffer, and what is terrible in life goes on somewhere behind the scenes. . . . And such a state of things is evidently necessary. . . . It is a general hypnosis. . . . That night I came to understand that I too had been contented and happy. . . . Freedom is a boon, I used to say, it is as essential as air, but we must wait awhile. Yes, that's what I used to say, and now I ask: why must we wait? (IX, 163)

Ivan concludes that he is too old now to combat the suffering around him, but he pleads with Alekhin to do something greater and more rational than simply to attain personal happiness. "Do good!" he advises (IX, 164).

However, neither Alekhin nor Burkin is visibly moved by Ivan's proselytizing. His final admonition to them shows that he is ignorant of the vital role beauty plays in their values, and they can only think:

it was tedious to listen to the story of the poor devil of a clerk who ate gooseberries. One felt like talking about elegant people, about women. . . . and the fact that lovely Pelageya was noiselessly moving about—that was better than any story. (IX, 164)

This point is further underlined in the next story, "About Love," in which Alekhin describes how he futilely denied himself beauty and happiness with another man's wife "in order to do good."

III "About Love" 1898

Alekhin's physical description in "Gooseberries" points to a contrast between his soiled peasant attire and his outward appearance, which looks "more like a professor or artist than a gentleman farmer." "About Love" further explores the contradictions in Alekhin's life, opposing the sterility of his outwardly "noble" existence to his poetic inward yearnings.

Alekhin begins his story with an exposition that accounts for the life that he has adopted and that is apparently so unsuited to him. Alekhin did not choose to become a farmer, but rather was forced into this role by his late father's heavy debts. He speaks of his life of physical toil with humorous disgust, commenting, "I myself plowed and sowed and reaped, and found it awfully tedious, and frowned with disgust, like a village cat driven by hunger to eat cucumbers in the kitchen garden (IX, 167). Unlike Tolstoi's character Levin in *Anna Karenina*, it is evident that Alekhin sees nothing noble in a "return to simplicity."

Alekhin then proceeds to relate his disappointment in love, which is presented in such a way that it becomes an indirect attack on Tolstoi's philosophy of the sanctity of marriage. Alekhin meets Anna Alekseevna and her husband, Luganovich, while he is serving in a temporary position as honorary Justice of the Peace. The friendship between Alekhin and the Luganovich family deepens over the years, as does the secret love between him and Anna. Yet as his title of "justice of the Peace" might indicate, Alekhin resists the temptation to marry Anna because it would "rudely break up the even course of the life of her husband, her children and the whole household. . . . Would it be honorable? . . . And how long would our happiness last? . . . and she apparently reasoned the same way" (IX, 171).

It is only when Anna's husband is transferred to another province and she and Alekhin must part for the last time that they finally confess their feelings for each other. At this moment Alekhin says he experienced an epiphany:

With a burning pain in my heart I realized that when you love, you must start from what is higher, more important than happiness or unhappiness, sin or virtue in their usual meaning, or you must not reason at all. (IX, 173)

Thus three different men have proposed contradictory solutions to avoid the isolation and futility of *futliarnost'*. Burkin advises against an excessive conformity to generalized, rigid rules at the expense of personal happiness, Ivan exposes the dangers of blindness to any consideration but one's own personal fulfillment, and Alekhin's tale illustrates the fallacy of total commitment to duty at the expense of the highest value, love. And although the perspective in all three stories differs, each narrative illustrates *futliarnost'*. The fact that this concept is capable of assuming many forms while retaining its basic characteristics underlines the need for self-scrutiny in order to avoid "life in a shell."

IV "The Darling" 1898

Chekhov called "The Darling" a humorous story, yet critics have responded to it with a variety of interpretations that indicate the subtlety of Olenka's characterization in this work. Tolstoi himself appreciated the satirical wit in "The Darling," but added that in Olenka Chekhov had unwittingly created a heroine who was "not ridiculous, but a wonderfully holy being."[2] He concluded with approval that Chekhov had unconsciously rejected his earlier notions of woman's emancipation, although this statement is clearly refuted by Chekhov's last story "The Bride."

The modern critic Renato Poggioli[3] also conceives of Olenka's total passivity and lack of discretion in love as a positive characteristic. Poggioli views Chekhov's story as an adaptation of the myth of Eros and Psyche, noting "that even in the profane prose of life there may lie hidden poetry's sacred spark."[4] Olenka is called "dusshechka," a diminutive of the Russian word "soul" (dusha), which links her with Psyche, whose Greek name also means "soul." The Psyche myth relates how the god Eros admonished her not to look upon him, and how she, curious to see her lover, breaks his command. Eros is infuriated and abandons Psyche, thus implying that love must be blind in order to endure. Poggioli deduces from this that Olenka's noncritical attitude toward the men she loves is far wiser than the curiosity displayed by Psyche, her Greek counterpart.

Still, such critics as Thomas Winner and Karl Kramer[5] have noted that these interpretations ignore the immaturity and even the despotism that Olenka exercises in her relationships. She is certainly not idealized by Chekhov, who appreciates her warmth and good nature, yet pokes fun at Olenka's four love relationships that are in many ways absurd and that constitute her only claim to identity.

The opening paragraph of "The Darling," in which Olenka is introduced to the reader, is constructed with a combination of details that immediately draw attention to her childlike identity. It is first established that she is the daughter of a retired collegiate assessor, and although it is mentioned that Olenka is "deep in thought" (IX, 200), the next sentence explains that these thoughts are only about the relief evening will bring from flies and the heat.

The next paragraph introduces Olenka's future husband Kukin, the despairing manager of a local theater, whom she loves with pity and maternal solicitude. Kukin's attraction to Olenka appears to be directed more toward her plump good looks than toward an appreciation of her devotion to him. "He proposed to her, and they married. And when he had a good look at her neck and her plump, firm shoulders, he struck his hands together, and exclaimed, 'Darling!' " (IX, 201). The romanticism of Kukin's feelings toward Olenka is further undercut by his mood after the wedding: "He was happy, but as it rained on their wedding day and the night that followed, the expression of despair did not leave his face" (IX, 201).

In fact, although it is clearly stated that Olenka and her new husband "got on well together," it is also mentioned that "Olenka was gaining weight and beamed with happiness, but Kukin was getting thinner and more sallow and complained of terrible losses, although business was fairly good" (IX, 202). These two statements are not mutually exclusive as they might appear to be at first glance: Olenka's maternal solicitude only encourages her husband's indulgent self-pity, and thus her love becomes fatal to him.

Chekhov's deliberately comic wording of the telegram informing Olenka of Kukin's death foreshadows his attitude toward her subsequent behavior: "Ivan Petrovich died suddenly today awaiting prot instructions funnyral Tuesday." The misspelled word "funnyral," in Russian *Pokhorony*, has associations with laughter, and the incomprehensible word *prot* adds to the absurdity of the telegram. Olenka proceeds to sob folk laments (My precious! Why did we ever meet? Why did I get to know you and to love you?" IX, 203), dresses in black, and after three months of grief marries again after a two-day romance.

Olenka's second husband Pustovalov impresses her as appearing "more like a landowner than a business man" (IX, 203). She respects him for his substantial appearance and for his fatherly advice to her that "if one of our dear ones passes on, then it means that this was the will of God, and in that case we must keep ourselves in hand and bear it submissively" (IX, 203). Her marriage to him is every bit as satisfying to Olenka as the relationship she had cherished with Kukin: she becomes involved with Pustovalov's lumber business to the same degree that she had earlier devoted herself to Kukin's theater, she adopts her new husband's "sedate and reasonable manner" (IX, 205) with the same abandon that she had earlier responded to Kukin's emotionalism, and she is equally bereaved when after six years of marriage to Pustovalov, he suddenly dies.

Again there follows a period of mourning in Olenka's life, this time lasting six months, which is characterized by the same folk laments and by the black clothing she donned after Kukin's death. Yet when Olenka begins to talk only of the veterinary business, and is seen happily doting on her veterinary boarder, it is clear that she has found another love to give meaning to life. But unlike her first two husbands "Volodichka" resents her total identification with him and admonishes her, "I've asked you before not to talk about things that you don't understand. When veterinarians speak among themselves please don't butt in! It's really annoying!" (IX, 206). Olenka's "happiness" with the veterinary does not last long in any case: he is transferred away with his regiment and she is left totally abandoned.

Yet Olenka arrives at perhaps her most perfect fulfillment in life when the veterinary returns and leaves his small son Sasha in her care:

She now had opinions of her own . . . saying that studying in high school was hard on the children, but that nevertheless the classical course was better than the scientific one because a classical education opened all careers to you . . . How she loves him! Not one of her former attachments was so deep; never had her soul surrendered itself so unreservedly, . . . and with such joy as now when her maternal instinct was increasingly asserting itself. For this little boy who was not her own . . . she would have laid down her life . . . with tears of tenderness. Why? But who knows why? (IX, 208 - 209)

There is an intimation that Olenka's total surrender to her love for Sasha will be her final undoing. Her domination over the boy is constantly threatened by the return of his mother, and from the last line of the story it is evident that the boy himself has dreams of rebellion. Olenka's doting love stifles Sasha, who sometimes expresses those emotions of independence in his sleep that will later be directed toward Olenka: "I'll give it to you! Scram! No fighting!" (IX, 210).

V   "Lady With a Lapdog" *1899*

After reading this story Gorky made the following remark: "Do you know what you are doing? You are killing realism. And you will kill it soon. Kill it for good. This form has outlived its time. It's a fact. After you no one can travel this road. No one can write so simply about such simple things as you do. After any of your insignificant stories everything seems crude, as though it were written not with a pen but with a log of wood. And the main thing, everything seems not simple enough, nor true."[6]

What did Gorky mean by his statement that Chekhov was killing realism? The story seems realistic enough: two people meet at a summer resort and fall in love. At first it is only a passing diversion to them, but later they discover that they are unable to forget each other and so begin to lead a double life. In summary it sounds like any banal love story.

But the essence of the story does not lie in the plot nor in its realistic quality. This realism is being killed, as Gorky said, because the story appeals to the imagination.

The opening sentence not only gives a full picture of a summer resort with its gossip, boredom, and people looking for adventure, it also unites the hero, Gurov, with the resort crowd. The second sentence shows the lady, separate from the crowd, walking with her white dog. As Gurov's relationship with Anna develops, his sense of identity shifts from an immersion in the superficial world of appearances to an inner, poetic perception of life which he associates with Anna. Through Gurov's love for Anna, her separation from the crowd is transferred onto a symbolic level: it is no longer merely physical, but metaphysical; not only temporary, but permanent. To the crowd Anna will always remain a lady with a lapdog. To Gurov she will become the embodiment of all that is beautiful in life.

"The Lady With a Lapdog" is structured upon two contrasting settings. The first two chapters of the story describe the nature of Gurov's initial attraction to Anna and his brief affair with her in Yalta. When he first sees Anna, Gurov reacts coolly: "If she is here without a husband and without friends," figured Gurov, "it wouldn't be a bad idea to get acquainted with her" (IX, 236). Chekhov uses the calculating, prosaic "figured" to underline the lack of any poetic element in this man. Gurov is bored and in search of a short, enjoyable liaison with a woman. However, Chekhov adds some information about Gurov's background that indicates that he once had romantic longings. He is a philologist by education and at one time was preparing to sing in a private opera. There is also an indication that Anna will touch some other chord in his unloving heart. The closing sentence of this chapter is: "But there is something pitiful in her," he thought, and began to fall asleep (IX, 238).

The second chapter deals with adultery and is built on small details. Anna's eyes sparkle and she loses her lorgnette through which she views the world. Gurov looks around after kissing her to see if anyone had seen his action. There is a lyrical epiphany; when sitting by the ocean with Anna, Gurov feels that "everything, if properly understood, would be entirely beautiful." A single candle barely illumines Anna's unhappy, guilty face after she has become Gurov's mistress.

Anna's remorse following adultery is reminiscent of the Anna-Vronsky scene in *Anna Karenina:*

It's not right. You're the first person not to respect me . . . God forgive me! I am a wicked woman. I despise myself, and have no desire to justify myself! It isn't my husband I have deceived, but myself! My husband may be a good, honest man but he is also a flunky! (IX, 239-240)

Chekhov undercuts the scene by having Gurov nonchalantly eat a piece of watermelon during Anna's tearful outburst, and by allowing him to comfort her so that "she was happy again, and they both began to laugh" (IX, 240).

Chapter 3 portrays Gurov's superficial life in Moscow and contrasts it with the lyrical memories he associates with Anna. The rounds of dinners, card games, and conversations no longer distract Gurov from his loneliness. He becomes painfully aware of a lack of communication with other people. This lack is summed up in a conversation between Gurov and an acquaintance to whom he says, "If you only knew what a charming woman I met in Yalta." His friend responds, "You are right. The sturgeon did have a slight smell" (IX, 244). The total poverty of Gurov's emotional life serves as an incentive in his decision to see Anna again.

Gurov's and Anna's reunion is described using a combination of details that parallel earlier observations and draw attention to the changes in their relationship. The description of Anna as "a little, undistinguished woman, lost in a provincial crowd, with a vulgar lorgnette in her hand" (IX, 245) contrasts with her romantic image in chapter 2 after she has just lost her lorgnette because embellishing Anna's appearance is no longer important to Gurov. He loves her as she is. As opposed to Gurov's relaxed cynicism in the first two chapters, he is now nervous and can only murmur, "But do understand, Anna, do understand" (IX, 246). The change in Gurov's feelings is also revealed in that he kisses Anna despite the two schoolboys who are watching, whereas earlier he had made conscious effort to conceal their relationship.

Like chapter 2, in which the seduction takes place, the last chapter is set in a hotel room. Though the social barriers still stand between Anna and Gurov, their feelings for each other and their attitude toward judgment from the outside world have changed. Whereas Anna first wept guiltily because she had committed the sin of adultery, she now cries with the pain of love, "out of sheer agitation, in the sorrowful consciousness that their life was so sad." Gurov is no longer indifferent to Anna's suffering, but shares in it: "Formerly in moments of sadness he had soothed himself with whatever logical arguments came into his head, but now he no longer cared for logic; he felt profound compassion, he wanted to be sincere and tender" (IX, 248).

The comfort that Anna and Gurov give each other unites them despite the many obstacles barring their happiness.

Anna Sergeevna and he loved each other as people do who are very close and intimate, like man and wife, like tender friends; it seemed to them that Fate itself had meant them for one another, and they could not understand why he had a wife and she a husband. . . . They forgave each other what they were ashamed of in their past, they forgave everything in the present, and felt that this love of theirs had altered them both. (IX, 249)

Although there is no realistic solution to their problem, at least Anna and Gurov know that their pain and sorrow, as well as their love, would always be shared.

VI "The Bishop"

Nils Ake Nilsson points out in his book *Studies in Chekhov's Narrative Technique*[7] the stylistic and thematic unity between "The Steppe" and "The Bishop." These two works are related by their narrative construction composed of short, distinct episodes that together create a revealing psychological portrait. Whereas in "The Steppe" Egor is discovering the world around him through the clash between his imaginative assertions and reality, in "The Bishop" Peter attempts to understand death despite the estrangement that renders the real imaginary to him.[8]

The story begins on the eve of Palm Sunday, describing the ill Bishop Peter's thoughts and perceptions as he distributes willows to the congregation. The bishop is isolated from the people around him, which is underlined by the use of the impersonal expression *emu kazalos'*, meaning "it seemed to him." The congregation seems "to heave like a sea" (IX, 287), and when an old woman appears before him, who to all appearances is his mother, he cannot believe in her reality.

Suddenly, as though in a delusion, it seemed to the Bishop that he saw Mariya Timofeevna, his own mother, whom he had not seen in nine years, coming up to him in the crowd, or perhaps it was only an old woman who resembled his mother. (IX, 287)

The bishop starts to cry at this moment for reasons unknown to himself, but which are probably related to his subconscious belief that he will soon die.

The bishop's estrangement from his personal identity is further indicated by his identification with the whole of nature, and even with objects. After Peter leaves the church he is soothed by the joyous chimes of the church bells, and feels that "white walls, white crosses on the tombs, white birches and black shadows—all these things seemed to be living their own lives, remote and incomprehensible, and very close to mankind" (IX, 288).

Upon returning to the monastery, Peter joyfully learns that the woman who had reminded him of his mother was indeed she, yet he is irritated to hear that he will not be able to see her until the following day. As in the church, he becomes increasingly aware of his physical discomfort: "His legs and arms were stiff, the back of his neck ached. He felt hot and uncomfortable" (IX, 289). Yet this mood dissolves as Peter becomes immersed in memories, which give him the same feeling of edification as his earlier identification with "incomprehensible things":

Dear, precious, unforgettable childhood! Why was it that those far-off days, which would never return, seemed brighter, gayer and richer than they really were! . . . And now prayers mingled with memories which shone ever more luminously like a flame . . . In summer they would take the icon in procession . . . and to the Bishop it seemed as though the air itself had trembled with joy as he followed behind the icon, barefoot, and hatless, with a simple smile on his lips and a simple faith in his heart. . . ." (IX, 289)

The present reality is unescapable and Father Sisoi's snoring in the next room "somehow suggested loneliness, forlornness, a strange wandering." When Father Sisoi enters to inform the bishop that it is time for matins, Peter confesses, "I can't sleep . . . I must be ill. I don't know what it is—Fever!" (IX, 290).

Nilsson notes in *Studies in Chekhov's Narrative Technique* that chapter 2 begins in a journalistic style, communicating Bishop Peter's routine existence.[9] Even the lunch with Peter's mother is a dry, formal affair, for she reacts to him more as to a bishop than as to a son. In response to Peter's sincere comment about how he has missed her while abroad, his mother can only say "Thank you" in the same tone as any one of his humble petitioners. Peter's feelings of warmth and joy in his mother's presence abruptly vanish. Again he experiences the painful consciousness of his estrangement from reality, and becomes aware of his physical malaise:

Abruptly the Bishop's mood changed. He gazed at his mother and could not understand how she had come by that timid, deferential expression of face and voice, and he could not understand what lay behind it . . . He felt sad and hurt. He was still suffering from the headache of the day before, and his legs were aching horribly, and the fish he was eating seemed stale and insipid, and all the time he was very thirsty. (IX, 292)

Bishop Peter becomes increasingly irritated when later that night he overhears the inane conversation between his mother, who keeps saying "We drank tea" (IX, 293), and Father Sisoi, who spouts absurd racial theories about the Japanese. When Father Sisoi finally enters the bishop's room later that night, Peter complains of the same illness as the night before, and the priest responds with similar behavior. He rubs the bishop with tallow, and starts to complain, which is of little comfort to Peter.

Chapter 3 reintroduces a journalistic style, further describing the bishop's reaction to his daily routine. Peter is distressed by the ignorance and cowardice of his suppliants, and is bored with useless documents and the reports he is obliged to write. As on Palm Sunday's eve, the ringing of the church bells has a joyful connotation for Peter, and in church he "felt not sorrow over his sins, nor any grief, only a great sense of peace and tranquility, and in his imagination he was being swept back into the distant past, to the days of his childhood and youth . . . The past rose up before him, vivid, beautiful, and joyful, as in all likelihood it had never been. And perhaps in the other world, in the life to come, we shall remember the distant past, our life on earth, with the same feeling. . . . He had faith, but something was not clear to him. Something was lacking, and he did not want to die" (IX, 295). The bishop weeps as he did in church on Palm Sunday, and it would seem that it is not only his death, but also the fact that there is no one "to whom he could unburden his soul," that is responsible for his misery.

Chapter 4 begins with a description of the weather after Mass on Thursday morning that echoes the optimism of the night after the Palm Sunday Mass:

When the service was over and the people had gone home, the warm sun was shining merrily, the water was streaming noisily in the gutters and the perpetual trilling of the larks came floating in from the fields outside the city, speaking of peace and tenderness. The trees were already awakening and smiling a welcome, and over them stretched the unfathomable, the immeasurable blue sky. (IX, 295)

Juxtaposed to this is the bishop's pain, isolation, and weariness, which are only relieved when he is saying Mass, and thus conscious of his sense of identity in the church:

His father had been a deacon, his grandfather a priest, his great-grandfather a deacon, and perhaps his whole family from the days when Christianity first entered Russia had belonged to the Church, and his love for the holy services, for the priesthood and for the sound of church bells was ineradicably born in him. In church, especially when he was conducting the service, he felt vividly alive, vigorous, and happy. So it was with him now. (IX, 297)

The bishop returns home after Mass to die. Again he is oppressed by the monastery as well as by Father Sisoi's banality, and feels relief at the hemorrhaging that signals the end of his life: "He felt that he was becoming thinner and weaker and more insignificant than anyone in the world, and it seemed to him that everything that had ever happened in the past was vanishing into the distance and would never come back again. 'How good!' he thought, 'Oh, how good' " (IX, 299).

When his mother sees Peter close to death, she at last forgets that he is a bishop and "She kissed him as though he were a child very close and dear to her." However, her gentle motherly action is not real to Peter, who already identifies himself with the world of nature where "he imagined himself a simple, ordinary fellow striding joyfully across the fields, swinging his cane, free as a bird to wander wherever he pleased under the broad spaces of the sunlit sky" (IX, 299).

The bishop dies on Saturday, a week after the story was begun. Yet nothing has changed: the church bells still ring on Easter morning, nature is beautiful, and people go about their business. Peter's last thoughts that he has finally been released from his identity as a bishop are confirmed, for hardly anyone remembers him:

A month later a new bishop was installed, and no one gave a thought to Bishop Peter. Soon he was completely forgotten. His old mother, who is living today in a remote little country town with her son-in-law the deacon, goes out toward evening to bring her cow in, and sometimes she will pause and talk with the other women in the fields about her children and grandchildren and her son who became a bishop, and she speaks very softly and shyly, afraid that no one will believe her. (IX, 300)

The reality from which the bishop felt so isolated toward the end of his life is indeed negligibly affected by his absence. And yet Peter's spirit seems to hover over those things he loved best. In the description of Easter morning the reader feels his eternal presence in the church bells and in the "quivering in the spring air."

VII "The Bride"

Chekhov's last story, "The Bride," is considered by most Soviet critics to be the sum of his creativity.[10] The following passage is most often cited as proof of the socialist implications underlying the heroine's decision to reject her bourgeois origins:

Oh, if only this new pure life would come more quickly, a life where one could look one's fate in the eyes boldly and straightforwardly, sure of being right, joyful and free! The time would come when there would be nothing left of her grandmother's house, that house where everything was so arranged that the four servants could only live in the basement in a single filthy room. (IX, 315)

A closer examination of Nadya's character will reveal the irony in this interpretation, for she herself is a dreamer who frequently becomes disillusioned with her impassioned statements. Throughout the story Nadya is involved in a process of self-discovery that by its very nature involves the formulation of dreams and subsequently the consideration of their ability to withstand the stress of reality.

First Nadya rejects her mother, then her fiancé, then Sasha, and it would seem possible that she might also modify her dreams of a social utopia.

The initial conflict preoccupying Nadya is introduced in the opening paragraph with the contrasting images of the Shumins' garden and their kitchen. Opposed to the world of the kitchen, which is intimately related to Nadya's past and her "passionate dream of marriage . . . ever since she was sixteen," is the world of the garden. There it is dark and peaceful and there the expanse of sky and land stretching out toward the unknown inspires dreams "full of riches and holiness" (IX, 301).

From the garden where Nadya is standing she can see the dining room where her "grandmother is bustling about in a magnificent silk dress" while her future father-in-law and fiancé speak with Nadya's mother. Nadya is surprised at how young her mother seems in the evening light, an observation which draws attention to Nadya's tendency to perceive things impressionistically, and to evaluate them according to her mood.

It is clear from the beginning that Nadya's marriage will force her to choose between the worlds of the garden and the kitchen, for her passive, domestic fiancé definitely belongs to the latter sphere. There is little passion or imagination in Nadya's feelings for Andrei. Later that night in her "uncomfortable soft bed" Nadya herself notes that she "had accepted him and gradually learned to appreciate this good and intelligent man" (IX, 304). Nadya is troubled by her lack of love for Andrei and somehow associates him with the languid, heavy night that seems to be suffocating her:

Through the big old-fashioned window she could see the garden, and beyond the garden lay the lilac bushes heavy with bloom, drowsy and languid in the cold air, and a heavy mist suddenly swept up to the lilacs, as though determined to drown them. The drowsy rooks were cawing in the distant trees. "My god, why am I so depressed?" Perhaps all brides feel the same before their weddings? (IX, 305)

Early the next morning Nadya again visits the garden, where nature inspires her with its beauty:

The night watchman had stopped tapping long ago. The birds were twittering beneath her window, and in the garden the mist vanished so that everything glittered and seemed to be smiling in the spring sunshine. Soon the whole garden, warmed and caressed by the sun, sprang to life, and drops of dew gleamed like jewels on the leaves; and the ancient, long neglected garden looked young and beautifully arrayed in the morning light. (IX, 305)

But the interval between the night watchman's tapping and the beginning of the morning routine is all too brief. After Granny awakens and the servants set up the samovar the hours pass slowly.

Nadya's alienation is heightened by an absurd conversation with Nina Ivanovna, which makes it clear to her that her mother "did not understand her, and was incapable of understanding her. She had never felt this way before, and it frightened her. She wanted to hide, and went back to her room." Later in the afternoon she is likewise disillusioned with Andrei, who seems in his element eating one boring meal after another and mouthing cliché romantic phrases to her:

"My dear, beautiful darling," he murmured. "Oh, how happy I am! I am out of my mind with happiness!" And it seemed to her that she had heard these same words long ago or perhaps she had read them somewhere . . . in an old dog-eared novel thrown away a long time ago. (IX, 307)

On the other hand Sasha's constant advice to her to go away to study and to become one of those people who is committed to a magnificent future has increasing appeal to Nadya. Sasha's dreams of a utopian society evoke the same emotional response as the garden, where horizons are limitless:

Only the enlightened and holy people are interesting—they are the only ones needed. The more such people there are, the quicker will the Kingdom of Heaven descend on earth. Then it will happen little by little that not one stone will be left standing, in this town of yours everything will be shaken to its foundations, and everything will be changed, as though by magic. "What a strange naive person he is" thought Nadya, "and those dreams of his—those marvelous gardens and glorious fountains—how absurd they are!" But . . . she found so much that was beautiful in his naiveté and his absurdity and the moment she permitted herself to dream of going away and studying, cold shivers bathed her whole heart and breast, and she was overwhelmed with sensations of joy and ecstasy. (IX, 306)

Chapter 3 is the turning point in the story, when Nadya finally rejects the "world of the kitchen" and her future husband along with it. Preparations for the wedding are described as oppressive to

Sasha, and it is as if nature affirms this opinion: "The summer had turned cold and wet, the trees were damp, the garden looked somber and uninviting, and none of this caused anyone to desire to work. . . . The fuss irritated Sasha . . ." (IX, 307-308).

Nadya feels horribly stifled in the new apartment her fiancé has decorated with vulgar paintings and pretentious middle class furniture: "All the time she felt weak and conscience-stricken, hating these rooms and beds and armchairs, nauseated by the painting of the naked woman. Already it had become transparently clear to her that she no longer loved Andrei Andreich . . ." (IX, 308).

The last two chapters deal with Nadya's life after she has rejected marriage to Andrei. Chapter 4 describes a confrontation between Nadya and her mother, in which Nina Ivanovna first tries to convince her daughter that marriage to Andrei is acceptable because "In nature there are always these transformations." Yet Nadya rejects this advice, and her mother admits that she herself wants to "live—to live!" (IX, 310) In contrast to her initial impression of Nina Ivanovna at the beginning of the story, Nadya now sees her mother as "older, uglier, and shorter than ever on that stormy night" (IX, 310).

Nadya decides to leave with Sasha and to follow his advice to study at the university. Chapter 5 describes her secret departure from the town and her joy at discovering new freedom.

When chapter 6 opens autumn and winter have already passed. Nadya has studied for a year, after which she returned to Moscow to visit Sasha who no longer inspires the same worshipful respect in her. She realizes now that he is provincial and lazy.

After this visit Nadya returns home, and she is shocked that the town is so much smaller and more dusty than she had remembered. Her soft, comfortable bed seems doubly absurd, and her mother's artificial philosophical statements even more precious. Even the telegram announcing Sasha's death does not seem real to Nadya, and she cannot react emotionally to it:

It hurt her that her foreboding and her thoughts about Sasha did not distress her, as once they would have done. She passionately wanted to live and she longed to be in St. Petersburg, and her friendship with Sasha, although still sweet, seemed to belong to a far distant past. (IX, 316)

Nadya has thus rejected dreams that centered first around her family, and then around Sasha. She is caught up in visions of "the bold new future," but whether this philosophy will also fail her is left ambiguous. Nadya seems more attracted by her imaginary conceptions of life than by reality itself, as is underlined in the penultimate paragraph of the story: "In her imagination life stretched before her, a new, vast, infinitely spacious life, and this life, though still obscure and full of mysteries, lured and attracted her" (IX, 316).

When Nadya leaves the town the next day she is full of high spirits and "expected never to return" (IX, 316). Still, the impression is created that further disillusionments await her.

CHAPTER 7

Chekhov's Plays

CHEKHOV wrote his first plays at the age of eighteen, but all that survived of those efforts are the titles: a drama *Without Fathers*, a comedy *Laugh It Off If You Can*, and a one-act comedy *Diamond Cuts Diamond*. (These titles are mentioned by Chekhov's eldest brother, Aleksandr, in a letter of October 14, 1878.) The manuscript of the earliest preserved play by Chekhov was discovered after his death and published in 1923. Because of the missing title page it was published as *A Play without A Title*,[1] but later it was named *Platonov* after the play's main character. Although the manuscript is undated there is evidence that the play was written in 1881, since Chekhov's brother Mikhail refers to it in his introduction to the second volume of Chekhov's letters. Apparently Chekhov took this play to the then-famous actress Mariya Yermolova with hopes that it would be performed at the Maly Theatre, and its rejection caused him great disappointment.

The play lacks artistic merit. It is too long, melodramatic, and as Mikhail wrote, "unwieldly," but it does offer interesting material for a study tracing some of Chekhov's themes and characters to their original sources. It is also significant as Chekhov's first effort to portray those sociological problems and conflicts that resulted from the emancipation of the serfs in the last two decades of the nineteenth century.

As in any period of transition there was uncertainty and confusion among the land-owning class, and many felt a helpless frustration at their inability to cope with change. Platonov, formerly a rich landowner and now a village teacher, is, in the words of one of the characters, "an admirable representative of our modern uncertainty."

To escape his frustration, Platonov involves himself with different women. Married to Sasha, a pious and innocent woman, he is having an affair with Anna, a general's widow. On discovering this, Sasha throws herself under a train, but is saved by the horse thief

126

Osip. In the third act, she finds out that her worthless husband has also been trying to revive his old love for Sonya, who viewed him in her student days as a second Byron.

Sonya decides to "save" Platonov, and she offers him a new, meaningful life with her: "I'll make a worker out of you. We'll be decent people, Mikhail. We shall eat our own bread. We shall live by the sweat of our brows. We shall have calloused hands. I shall work, Mikhail" (p. 116). Platonov agrees to this scheme without much conviction or enthusiasm, but just as he prepares to leave, he is summoned to court "in the case of an assault committed upon the person of Mariya Grekhova daughter of Councellor of State." The summons does not deter Platonov, but at this point he finds it convenient to spend two weeks with Anna, prior to leaving with Sonya forever.

The last act is filled with every theatrical cliché and melodramatic device possible. Sasha poisons herself with matches, Sonya throws herself on her knees in the presence of Anna and begs Platonov to leave with her, and Mariya Grekhova comes in to announce that she is withdrawing her summons and that she too loves Platonov.

Exasperated, Platonov vows to revenge himself on all these loving women: "They all love me. When I get well I'll corrupt you. Before I used to say nice things to them, but now I'm corrupting them all" (p. 162). Sonya relieves him from the necessity of fulfilling such an ambitious vow by shooting Platonov with a pistol and wounding him fatally. The play ends with a lament of Colonel Triletsky, Sasha's father: "The Lord has forsaken us. For our sins. For my sins. Why did you sin, you old jester? Killed God's own creatures, drank, swore, condemned people . . . The Lord couldn't put up with it any more and struck you down" (p. 165)."

Such lamentations were not part of Chekhov's later art, but the spiritual bankruptcy, the destructive forces of ennui, and the idea that work is man's salvation were to become some of his recurring themes. The figure of a bored, impoverished landowner unable to revive his youthful ideals and resentful of any efforts to save him appears again in Chekhov's next play, *Ivanov*.

I   Ivanov

It is apparent that Chekhov himself rejected *Platonov* so completely that he considered *Ivanov* his first play. In a letter to his brother Aleksandr in October of 1887 Chekhov said, "It is the first time I have written a play, ergo, mistakes are unavoidable. The plot is complicated and not stupid. I end each act like a short story. All the acts run on peacefully and quietly, but at the end I give the spectator a punch in the face. My entire energy is concentrated on a few really powerful and striking scenes; but the bridges joining them are insignificant, dull, and trite. Nevertheless, I am pleased, for however bad the play may be, I have I think, created a type of literary significance."[2]

The type Chekhov created was not new in Russian literature. Aside from the fact that Ivanov was a reworked version of Platonov, he was similar to many so-called superfluous men who dominated Russian novels since the early nineteenth century. Behind his melancholy, boredom, and cosmic fatigue stood his idealistic past, where his powers were directed toward passionate speeches about progress, human rights, and agricultural improvements. It is the discrepancy between what he had dreamed he would become and what he actually did become that lies at the source of his illness. As a part of his rebelliousness and youthful dreams, Ivanov married a Jewish girl, Sarah, who gave up her inheritance and her faith to become his wife. As the play opens, Sarah is suffering from tuberculosis, Ivanov's lands are mortgaged to Lebedev, and he himself is about to become involved with Sasha, a young and idealistic daughter of Lebedev who is bent on saving Ivanov. Chekhov said of Sasha (letter of Dec. 30, 1888 to Suvorin), "She is the type of female whom the males do not conquer by the brightness of their feathers, their fawning or their bravery, but by their complaints, their whining, their failures. She is a woman who loves a man at the moment of his downfall. The moment Ivanov loses heart, the girl is at his side. That was what she was waiting for . . . She is not in love with Ivanov but with that task of hers."[3]

Ivanov's relationship to his wife is seen and evaluated by different people: by common gossipers (act 2), by Dr. Lvov, by Sarah, and by Ivanov himself. The issue becomes a catalyst that reveals the degree of honesty each character has toward himself and others.

According to gossip, Ivanov is a murderer, a blood sucker, and a thief: an opinion that is a crude distortion of the truth. Dr. Lvov pronounces a similar judgment on Ivanov. Unlike the gossips, Lvov is motivated by sincere honesty and by a genuine concern for Sarah's health. Dr. Lvov correctly sees that Ivanov's lack of reaction to the fact that his wife is dying and his behavior with Sasha are largely responsible for Anna's death. Still, he fails to take into account Ivanov's idealistic past and his present ennui. Chekhov writes of the doctor: "He belongs to the type of honest, straightforward, excitable, but also narrow-minded and plain-spoken man."[4] As the count says of Lvov, he is "like a parrot who thinks of himself as a second Dobrolyubov." His role is thus a caricature of the liberal *narodnichestvo* (populism) dramas popular at the time.

Ivanov's reaction to Dr. Lvov is indicative of his attitude toward himself. Ivanov is not intentionally evil, but he feels himself powerless to resolve all the contradictions and complexities of his weak nature. Thus he admonishes Dr. Lvov for his harsh judgment, which is lacking in depth and perception:

No, doctor. We all have too many wheels and gears for us to be judged by first impressions or by a few external traits. I don't know you, you don't know me, and we don't know ourselves. Isn't it possible to be a good doctor—and at the same time not understand people? You'll have to admit that, unless you're blind. (p. 43)[5]

Although Ivanov does not fully accept Lvov's definition of him, he realizes that he alone is responsible for his life. Still he cannot reconcile himself to his present ennui:

I can stand all these things! Anxiety, depression, bankruptcy, the loss of my wife, premature old age, loneliness, but I just can't bear the contempt I have for myself. The shame that I, a strong, healthy man, have somehow become a kind of Hamlet, a Manfred, just about kills me! Oh, I know there are fools who are flattered when you call them a Hamlet, but to me it's an insult! It wounds my pride, I'm oppressed with shame, and I suffer . . . (p. 29)

Ivanov agrees with the doctor that his passivity is the indirect cause of both his wife's death and of his financial problem.

The dramatic action of this play is developed in accordance with the painful self-revelation which in the end drives Ivanov to suicide. Ivanov's psyche is revealed through his own remarks about himself, his gestures, his reactions, and the pauses in his speech.

Each act places an emphasis on Ivanov's estrangement from his surroundings. This is frequently comic, as in the contrast between Ivanov and Borkin, but it is just as often tragic. The comic episodes balance the tragic ones and serve as parodies, reflecting as if in a distorted mirror the plight of the main character. Both Count Shabelsky, Ivanov's uncle, and Lebedev, chairman of the County

Council, speak of their idealistic past with humor, yet Ivanov cannot feel indifferent to what he has become, and hence he suffers. Ivanov's relationship with Sasha is parodied by Shabelsky's vacillating intention to marry the rich young widow Babakina. Just like Ivanov, the count reasserts his honesty at the end of the play, telling Babakina he hates her. However, Ivanov must pay a tragic price to extricate himself from his marriage to Sasha. Lvov's aggressive honesty is a parody of what Berdnikov calls Ivanov's "subjective honesty." Although the doctor acts honorably, Ivanov's passive honesty enables him to judge himself and others with more insight than Lvov.

Chekhov wrote to Suvorin about *Ivanov* on January 7, 1889: "In the conception of Ivanov I hit approximately on the dot, but the performance is not worth a damn. I should have waited."[6] Chekhov's conception was to portray the "superfluous man" of the 1880s in all of his psychological complexity, but he had not yet mastered the dramatic subtleties of characterization. The excess of monologues and self-explanatory speeches in *Ivanov* kept it well within the bounds of the traditional theater, while Chekhov was striving to achieve something new. In a letter of October 10 - 12 to his brother Aleksandr he says of *Ivanov*, "Korsh hasn't found a single mistake or fault in it so far as stage technique is concerned which proves how good and sensible my critics are."[7] Korsh hadn't found a mistake because *Ivanov* conformed to the requirements of the conventional play.

Ivanov is certainly a vast improvement over *Platonov*. It is much more concise, and Chekhov realized the importance of ending each act definitely. At the end of the first act Sarah leaves her house to follow Ivanov, and at the end of the second act she appears at the very moment of Sasha's and Ivanov's kiss. The third act ends with Ivanov's rebuke to Sarah that she will soon die, and the fourth act with his suicide.

Chekhov failed to make an original creation out of a character that had become stock in Russian literature. As Suvorin said, "Ivanov was a ready-made man." Chekhov denied the charge and replied (February 8, 1889) that Ivanov was not static because he was "ready-made" but because the author's hands were unskillful. Chekhov obviously tried to portray the inner emotional life of his hero, but didn't know how to do it except with worn-out devices.

II   The Wood Demon

While Chekhov was writing *The Wood Demon* he was at the
same time at work on "A Boring Story." However, whereas "A Boring Story" displays all the control of an admirable craftsman, *The
Wood Demon* confirms Chekhov's own suspicion that he was not
yet a playwright. When the play was passed by the censor in October, 1889, it was rejected by the Literary-Theatrical Committee of
St. Petersburg, among whose members was Grigorovich. Lensky, an
actor of the Moscow Maly Theatre for whose benefit night the play
was submitted, wrote Chekhov two weeks later, "Write stories. You
are too scornful of the stage and the dramatic form. You respect
these things too little to write plays."[8] Nemirovich-Danchenko was
more charitable and more perceptive. He wrote, "You ignore too
many of the requirements of the stage, but I have not observed that
you scorn them; simply, rather, that you don't know what they
are."[9]

In December, Chekhov finally sold the play to the private
Abramov Theatre in Moscow, and it was presented on the Moscow
stage on December 27th. The criticism of the play was singularly
severe. The kindest review came from a magazine *The Actor*,
No. 6, 1890 which said, "Chekhov's talent, without a doubt, is above
the play he wrote, and the play's strange qualities are explained,
probably, by the speed of the work and a sad delusion regarding in-
escapable qualities of every dramatic work." Chekhov added his
personal criticism of *The Wood Demon*, which had also failed his
own artistic expectations. In a letter to Urusov, literary critic and
chairman of a drama society, he stated, "I cannot publish [*The
Wood Demon*]. I . . . am trying to forget it."[10] (The play was in
fact later revised and staged as *Uncle Vanya*.)

Chekhov did succeed in removing the conventional plot from
The Wood Demon, but he had not yet mastered the technique of
portraying inner psychological action. The play is too mechanical,
undisciplined, and verbose. The inner psychological moments
which in later plays would be depicted by a suggestive line of
speech or a mere gesture, are expressed in loud monologues or
bathetic dialogues. The play is also undermined by unconvincing
coincidences and melodramatic situations. Letters and diaries serve
to communicate information in a contrived manner, characters
appear on stage at the proper moments as if by chance, and in Act

Four a fire is created to get Khrushchev off stage. The play ends
with the clown Dyadin's remark which ironically defines not only
his own absurdity but also the play's: "That is delightful—Just
delightful" (p. 124).

The theme and characterization are developed in accordance
with the love relationships in the play. Serebryakov, an old and in-
sufferable professor, is married to a very young and beautiful
woman, Elena. The stupid boor Orlovsky and the Byronic rake
Fedor both crudely attempt to seduce Elena, but receive only moral
lectures for their pains.

Chekhov was obviously under the influence of Tolstoi's teachings
at this time. The passive but virtuous Elena delivers speeches on the
sanctity of marriage, purity, loyalty, and self-sacrifice. Although
Elena is unjustly maligned throughout the play she is inwardly
sustained by her false belief that she is the paragon of Russian
womanhood:

Oh, to be free as a bird, to fly away from all your drowsy faces and your
monotonous mumblings and forget that you've even existed at all! Oh, to
forget oneself and what one is . . . But I am a coward; I am afraid, and tor-
tured by my conscience. I know that if I were to be unfaithful, every other
wife would do the same thing and leave her husband, too. But then God
would punish me. If it weren't for my conscience, I'd show you how free
my life could be. (p. 96)

There is another love triangle between the professor's spoiled
daughter Sonya, the idealistic "wood demon" Dr. Khrushchev, and
the scoundrel Zheltukhin. Khrushchev eventually proposes to Sonya,
who accepts his offer, at which point she too starts mouthing
Tolstoian precepts: "There is no evil without some good in it. Our
sorrow has taught me that we must forget our own happiness and
think only of the happiness of others. Our lives should be a continual act of self-sacrifice" . . . (p. 113)

All the characters are united by the thematic leitmotif of their
wasted lives, and by their attempt to delude themselves with
rationalizing philosophy. The "wood demon" Khrushchev sums up
the lives of everyone in the play as follows:

We say that we are serving humanity, but at the same time we inhumanly
destroy one another. For instance, did you or I do anything to save George?
Where's your wife, whom we all insulted? Where's your peace of mind,
where's your daughter's peace of mind? Everything's been destroyed,
ruined. You call me a Wood Demon, but there's a demon in all of you.

You're all wandering lost in a dark forest, you're all groping to find a way in life. We know just enough and feel just enough to ruin our own lives and the lives of others. (p. 117)

Voinitsky has sacrificed his entire identity to Serebryakov, whom he has worshipped as a great genius for years, only to discover his mistake when it is too late. Serebryakov, whose entire youth was devoted to work, tries desperately to achieve happiness as an old man by exercising the power of his position, but he only succeeds in destroying those around him. Elena is proud of her "virtue," but she is a failure in her inability to love anyone and quite rightly defines herself as a "worthless, empty and quite pathetic woman" (p. 93). Fedor and Zheltukhin are leading senseless lives, and justifying themselves with cynicisms modeled after Lermontov's Byronic hero Pechorin.

Though *The Wood Demon* was a failure in terms of its artistry, its conception of form revealed the trend toward dramas of "inner action" which was to become fully actualized in Chekhov's later plays. *Uncle Vanya*, which was modeled after *The Wood Demon*, will give the most concrete example for studying the development of Chekhov's technique from banal melodrama to masterful dramatic art.

III   The Seagull

Perhaps it is fitting that after the failure of *The Wood Demon*, Chekhov would want to write a play about art and the nature of artists. *The Seagull* marks Chekhov's maturity as a playwright, and it is also the most innovative of his plays. Chekhov wrote *The Seagull* in 1895, and in a letter to Suvorin (October 21, 1895) he said that he was working on it with pleasure, "though I sin terribly against the conventions of the stage. It is a comedy with three female parts, six male, a landscape, a view of a lake, much talk about literature, little action, and five tons of love."[11]

It was the "sinning against convention" that was most probably responsible for the scandalous failure of *The Seagull* at its first performance on October 17, 1895. The play's initial engagement lasted only five days, and it was greeted with satirical invective from the St. Petersburg audience, as well as from the art critics who reviewed it. Very few people were astute enough to appreciate *The Seagull's* innovative use of mood, subtext, and symbolism as a new dramatic form.

The theme of *The Seagull* deals with the complex relationship between art, love, and life. Konstantin's play in the first act serves to polarize the characters' feelings around this subject, and to reveal the role of each individual in both a thematic and a dramatic sense.

At the beginning of *The Seagull* Masha, Medvedenko, and Polina are united by their total unconcern with the content of Treplev's play. They are all totally immersed in love conflicts and art has no relevance to their lives. On the other hand, for Sorin, who has failed in his ambitions to be a writer as well as in love; for Nina, who aspires to be a great actress; for Treplev's mother Arkadina, who is a famous actress; for the idealistic Dr. Dorn; and for the popular author Trigorin, there is an intimate relationship between art and personal identity.

Arkadina views her son Konstantin's attempt to create "new forms" in the theater as both a personal and a professional threat. Treplev is aware of his mother's animosity toward this assertion of his rebellious individuality, and he mockingly recites Queen Gertrude's lines to Arkadina before his play is performed. The oedipal power struggle between Konstantin and his mother is thus transferred onto the more abstract level of art, where it can be interpreted as the battle waged by every new generation to replace worn-out art forms.

Arkadina's lover, Trigorin, also feels no affinity for Konstantin's play. He confesses to understanding neither its abstract symbolism nor its emotional intensity. For Trigorin creative writing is not a dynamic process of discovery, but rather it is a rational process with a given methodology: "I take every word, every sentence I speak, and every word you say, too, and quickly lock them up in my literary warehouse—in case they might come in handy sometime" (p. 148). Like Arkadina, Trigorin desires to dominate the young, creative energy which he himself cannot generate. His destructive love relationship with Nina parallels Arkadina's power over her son.

Dorn is the only member of the "older generation" who truly understands, and sympathizes with Treplev's efforts. It is interesting that Dorn, who is an experienced man, shares the same abstract notion of art as the naive and alienated Konstantin. Dorn's remarks to Konstantin are supportive, but at the same time they offer valuable critical advice:

There must be a clear and definite idea in a work of art—you must know why you're writing—if not, if you walk along this enchanted highway without any definite aim, you will lose your way and your talent will ruin you. (p. 139)

Treplev asserts that "one must portray life not as it is, not as it should be, but as it appears to be in dreams" (p. 131). Nina replies that, on the contrary, art must express life's strongest emotion, love. Nina not only has a strongly idealistic vision of the role of love in art, she also sees it as paramount in the life of the artist himself. And, although Treplev and Nina disagree on the focus of art in human relationships, they are both united by their naive dreams and by the shock of reality they must suffer.

Nina's and Treplev's parallel struggle to overcome the frustrations of reality and to establish a real artistic identity is symbolized by the central image of the seagull Treplev has wantonly killed. The impetus for this symbol was an incident that occurred when Chekhov's friend Levitan and he were walking in the wood and Levitan shot a woodcock. Chekhov picked up the wounded bird and Levitan asked him to crush its head with a gun stock. Chekhov replied he could not do it, but Levitan continued to plead with him to end the bird's suffering. Chekhov wrote to Suvorin on April 8, 1892: "I had to obey Levitan and kill it. One more beautiful, enamored creature gone, while two fools went home and sat down to supper."[12]

Nina's identification with a seagull is mentioned when she first arrives at the Treplevs' in Act One. Although her family has forbidden her to visit there, she longs "for this lake, as if I were a seagull" (p. 130). Later, at the end of act 2, the writer Trigorin interprets the dead seagull as a premonition of Nina's own fate in love: "A young girl like you has lived in a house on the shore of a lake since she was a little girl; she loves the lake like a seagull. Then a man comes along, sees her, and having nothing better to do, destroys her like this seagull here" (pp. 150 - 151). When Nina's unhappy romance with Trigorin, as described in act 4, becomes an actualization of this "fiction," Nina associates her identity entirely with a wounded seagull and even signs her letters to Treplev "the seagull."

But Nina's dedication to art ultimately reverses her fate. In her last speech she declares her triumph to Konstantin with the following words:

I've become a real actress. I enjoy acting! I revel in it! The stage intoxicates me, and on it I feel very beautiful. While I've been here, I've spent a lot of time walking and thinking . . . thinking . . . and I feel that my spirit's growing stronger every day. I know now, Kostya, that what matters most for us, whether we're writers or actors, isn't fame or glamor, or any of the things I used to dream of. What matters most is knowing how to endure, knowing how to bear your cross and still have faith. I have faith now and I can stand my suffering when I think of my calling, I'm not afraid of life. (p. 174)

Thus, although Trigorin's interpretation of *The Seagull* correctly foretold Nina's tragedy in love, it failed to take into account her success as an artist.

On the other hand, the seagull assumes an entirely different symbolic meaning in terms of Trigorin's fate. In the second act Konstantin shoots the seagull as a demonstration of his failure in love, and as a symbolic act to Nina that he might be his own next victim. Thus, Konstantin's ultimate failure is ironically not in his unrequited love for Nina. Rather, it is the result of his inability to find a direction in art. In the last act Konstantin says to Nina of himself:

TREPLEV, *sadly*. You've found your road, you know where you're going—but I'm still floating about in a maze of dreams and images, without knowing what it is I am to do . . . I have no faith, and I have no calling. (p. 174)

Konstantin has become his own victim because he is caught between the power of his imagination to visualize and his impotence to actualize that vision into art. His final self-destructive frustration is resolved in the act of suicide, where his identification with the seagull becomes complete.

There are other symbols in the play that evoke different responses from the characters and are related to the thematic development. The lake on Arkadina's estate represents a promise of fulfillment: to Treplev it is associated with his play and with his love for Nina, to Trigorin it offers the solace of fishing (p. 168), and to Nina it is the lure that she will become a great actress. At the end of act 1 Dorn speaks to Masha of "sorcerer's lake," remarking on its power to evoke dreams. In the last act the lake's glassy surface is ruffled by chaotic, stormy winds, just as the dreams of each of the characters have been thrashed about by the forces of reality.

Flowers are also used as a symbol of the beauty and tender

fragility of dreams. Polina jealously destroys the flowers that Nina presents to Dorn (p. 145), which parallels Arkadina's attitude toward Treplev and Trigorin's attitude toward Nina. Trigorin speaks of his wasted dreams as being like "flowers, torn from their roots" (p. 148), and at the end of the play Nina reminds Treplev of their youth, when feelings were "like tender, exquisite flowers" (p. 175). In *The Seagull* it seems that flowers, like youthful dreams, are destined to be trampled on or destroyed by time and indifference.

There are no real dramatic climaxes in *The Seagull* until Treplev's suicide at the end of the play. The plot develops with the introduction of the major characters in act 1, focuses on the love triangles between Trigorin-Nina-Treplev, Nina-Trigorin-Arkadina, and Medvedenko-Masha-Treplev in acts 2 and 3, and shows the resolutions of these conflicts in act 4. At the end of the play Treplev has abandoned Nina to return to Arkadina, Masha has married Medvedenko although she still loves Treplev, and both Nina and Trigorin have been jilted. Chekhov did not even portray Nina's affair with Trigorin on the stage, but used the messenger technique to report it to Dr. Dorn, and thus to the audience, in act 4.

Both David Magarshack in his book *Chekhov the Dramatist* and Maurice Valency in *The Breaking String* emphasizes that *The Seagull* is the first of Chekhov's plays to use the dramatic technique of indirect action. Unlike *Ivanov* and *The Wood Demon*, where thoughts and ideas were revealed through standard plot developments, *The Seagull* highlights the more subtle psychological reactions of its characters through dialogue and symbolism.

Another innovation in *The Seagull* is Chekhov's wedding of comic and tragic elements. Although Arkadina's egoism, Treplev's fanatical attachment to his mother, and Trigorin's passion for fishing evoke a comic response, the reader understands each character too well to laugh without sympathy. The humor in *The Seagull*, which has its source in the frequent absurdity of human behavior, is never without a sadness that dreams very rarely come true. This thematic focus will be repeated in Chekhov's three later plays *Uncle Vanya*, *Three Sisters*, and *The Cherry Orchard*.

IV   Uncle Vanya

Having failed in the first two plays, Chekhov worked on *Uncle Vanya* without sharing his conception of it with anyone. Thus there are no indications anywhere as to when the play was written.

Chekhov mentions its existence for the first time in a letter to Suvorin dated December 2, 1886: "Two long plays have to be set up still; *The Seagull* which is known to you, and *Uncle Vanya*, which is not known to anyone in the world."

The play first appeared in the anthology of plays and then in a provincial theater, where it was an immediate success. Chekhov was surprised at the favorable reception of the play and wrote to his brother Mikhail on October 26, 1898:

> *My Uncle Vanya* is being performed throughout the provinces and is a success everywhere. So you see, one never knows where he'll make it and where he won't. I never counted on this play at all."[13]

It appeared first at the *Khudozhestvenny* (Art) Theatre in Moscow on October 26, 1899. The critics of the capital were impressed. It was said that in the play, "the terrible prose of life has been elevated into a chef d'oeuvre of poetry." Perceptive critics like Ignatev noticed the absence of action, and wrote that "*Uncle Vanya* is significant in that the heroes have no will, no goal, do not know whether the circumstances are profitable for them or not, nor what kind of behavior will be theirs in the next moment. They are passive . . . . Here the unity of action is substituted by the unity of mood."[14]

In fact, all but a few critics approved of the play. Tolstoi summed up the play in the following way to the actor A. A. Sanin, "Where is the drama? In what does it consist?"[15]

The action of *Uncle Vanya* consists of the movement from an established routine to the brief disturbance of that pattern, which contains a moment of illumination for the characters and a return to routine. The impetus for the shift in consciousness is the presence of Professor Serebryakov and his young wife Elena, whose extraordinary beauty arouses a longing for life in the others. Only they prove unequal to the challenge, and must deal with the failure of their dreams. The moment of illumination shows the characters that their inabilty to truly live has already determined not only their present, but their future, and this knowledge becomes an irrevocable part of their being. The question is no longer how to live, but as Voinitsky expresses it, "with what to fill the passing years?" (p. 216).

The themes of self-destruction and the violation of beauty are introduced at the beginning of act 1. In the opening scene, Dr. Astrov (the rewritten Dr. Khrushchev from *The Wood Demon*) asks the old

nurse, Marina, whether he has changed in the eleven years she has
known him. Her answer is the first expression of the theme which
will be restated throughout the play on different levels: "Oh yes.
You were young, handsome then, and now you seem like an old
man. And you drink too" (p. 178). The nurse uses the Russian word
krasota, "beauty," for "handsome," and it becomes a thematic leitmotif which is very prominent in the first two acts, subsides in the
third act, and is totally absent from the last act, except in Sonya's
final speech.

The two central images embodying physical beauty are the Russian forests and Elena. The idealistic Dr. Astrov plants new trees
every year because, as Sonya says:

He claims that forests beautify the earth, and so teach man to understand
the beautiful, and instill in him a feeling of respect and awe. Forests temper
the severity of the climate. In countries where the climate is warmer, less
energy is wasted on the struggle with nature and that is why man there is
more gentle and loving; the people there are beautiful, supple, and sensitive, their speech is refined and their movements graceful. (p. 185)

Astrov believes that man's creative and rational powers should be
devoted to the preservation of that which is aesthetic in the environment, so that in a thousand years' time the earth might still retain
its loveliness.

On the other hand, Vanya has a cynical attitude toward the
preservation of forests. He is much more interested in the utility of
the trees on his estate than in their beauty, and feels no compunc-
tion in burning logs in his fireplace or using wood for his barns. This
attitude is not surprising in view of his physical appearance, which
is described as "disheveled" (p. 179).

Both Astrov and Voinitsky are united in their love for the
beautiful Elena. When Astrov realizes that he is infatuated with
Elena he abandons his forest and medical practice to "seek her out
greedily" (p. 207). Yet Astrov's tragedy is that while his attraction to
Elena reveals his lack of a personal life, it does not involve his
emotions. At the beginning of the play he says, "I don't love
anyone" (p. 178), and this becomes the leitmotif which is confirmed
in the last scene. His parting kiss to Elena is one neither of love nor
of passion, but simply a gesture toward a momentarily aroused feeling that at one time in his life could have been real. Astrov's nature,
as indicated by his desire to heal and to preserve the beauty of

forests, is creative, yet he fails in the design of his own life.

Apparently Stanislavsky did not understand that point, for in his letter to Olga Knipper Chekhov writes in regard to the last scene:

In accordance with your orders I hasten to reply to your letter where you ask about the last scene of Astrov and Elena. You write that Astrov in that scene behaves with Elena as with someone madly in love, that he clutches at his feeling as a drowning man for straw. But this is incorrect, completely incorrect. Astrov likes Elena, she overwhelms him with her beauty, but in the last act he already knows that nothing will come of it, that Elena will disappear from him forever—and he talks with her in this last scene in the same tone of voice as the heat of Africa, and kisses her, just simply out of nothing to do. If Astrov plays this scene violently, then the entire mood of the fourth act will be destroyed. (September 30, 1899)[16]

In opposition to Astrov's character, Uncle Vanya could perhaps be called destructive. Astrov accuses him of harboring this quality in respect to the forests, and Elena remarks on it in regard to other people:

As Astrov said just now, see how thoughtlessly you destroy the forests, so that soon there will be nothing left on earth. In just the same way you recklessly destroy human beings, and soon, thanks to you, loyalty and purity and self-sacrifice will have vanished along with the woods. Why can't you look with calm indifference at a woman unless she belongs to you? Because . . . the doctor is right. You are all possessed by a devil of destructiveness; you have no feeling, no, not even pity, for either the woods or the birds or women, or for one another. (p. 187)

Yet just as Astrov fails to create, Uncle Vanya does not succeed in culminating his destructive impulses. He has already sacrificed the greater part of his life in a false dedication to the professor, who is a fraud. When Vanya becomes aware of the implications of his wasted life he attempts to shoot the professor and then himself. Both times he fails, and as a further insult to his masochistic pride, no one attempts to arrest him. Uncle Vanya is denied even the comfort of being thought of as a madman or a potential murderer; he is just a jester, devoid of any distinguishing personal trait. In his failure to destroy lies his inability ultimately to act out anything at all.

Uncle Vanya does not arouse anyone's sympathy. There is something comic in his love for Elena and in his homely dreams of a mediocre life with her. It is also obvious that while Elena responds to Astrov as a man, she does not to Uncle Vanya. Elena succeeds in resisting the temptation to consummate her attraction to Astrov, but in the best Freudian fashion takes his pencil as a souvenir of the possibility of an affair.

Astrov is said to be Chekhov's favorite character. Indeed, he is close to Chekhov in the lack of sentimentality with which he treats his profession as a doctor, in his lack of illusions, in his interest in alleviating the ills of Russia, in his desire to preserve the beauty in the world, and in his uncommitted personal life. (Chekhov wrote *Uncle Vanya* before he married Olga Knipper).

The secondary characters seem superfluous at first glance, and apparently add nothing to the action of the play. As in other Chekhov plays, they serve as distorting reflections of the main characters, parodying their essential traits. Marina's main function in life is to feed others: she is perfectly satisfied with the routine and is disturbed only when something interferes with it. After Sonya has been rejected by Astrov, she settles down in the same routine and her function in life becomes the feeding of others. Telegin gave his property for the sake of strangers (his wife's children); and Uncle Vanya, like Telegin, can say at the end of his life, "I did not forsake my duty." The irony in both cases lies in the fact that neither Uncle Vanya nor Telegin had any duty toward the people for whom they gave up their own lives and that thus they failed in their duty to themselves. Mariya Vasilevna, with her perennial reading and note taking in the margins of books, is a parody of Professor Serebryakov, who writes books that have as much value to others as reading does to Mariya herself. Marina, Telegin, and Mariya Vasilevna represent the unaware, who apparently settled into a pattern very early in life and who would never question its merits or the possibility of anything else. Juxtaposed to the indifference of these people are the longings of Uncle Vanya, Astrov, Elena, and Sonya. They too finally accept the routine of their lives. The difference is that they are conscious of their fate, whereas the other three remain ignorant.

Structurally *Uncle Vanya* is a very carefully wrought play. The particularly Chekhovian innovation is in the author's ability to combine all the elegiac elements and at some point to turn them into a comic situation. The tragic elements that constantly verge on the comic, and the ridiculous scenes that often inspire melancholy are probably what is meant by a special Chekhovian mood. It remains to examine how this particular mood is created. The details, though realistic in nature, make an appeal to the imagination. They illuminate the characters beyond their words and actions, and at times reveal their destiny. In addition, Chekhov uses landscape or simple objects for the same purpose of indirect dramatization.

Seemingly, nothing important is said in the opening lines of the play. On closer examination, it becomes obvious that those few lines already contain not only an introduction of the characters, but also the direction of the action and a hint of the outcome. The opening scene takes place in a garden. Cosy routine is indicated by the table set for tea; and the guitar, an accompaniment to the play, is there. It is cloudy. Marina offers tea to Astrov, and on his refusal, some vodka. To her offer he replies that he does not drink vodka every day. He adds that it is stifling. All these small details will receive amplification later: the cloudy weather will turn into a storm symbolic of the psychological storm gathering among the characters; it will be shown how the life on the estate is the kind that stifles human beings; and the vodka will become a means by which the self-destruction of Astrov will be accomplished.

Significantly, the insensitive characters do not notice the weather, so that the effect is one of two contrapuntal voices expressing the awareness and unawareness of the spiritual stifling. Upon entering, Serebryakov exclaims, "Superb, superb, what glorious views!" (p. 180); Voinitsky says, "It's hot and humid" (p. 180); and Telegin, the unconscious voice, says (although not in answer) "The weather is enchanting, the birds are singing, we all live in peace and harmony . . . what else do we want?" (p. 180). These remarks about the weather are a method of characterization, and they reveal as much about the characters as any of their speeches on profound subjects. Elena, who reconciles herself to life rather than actively reacting to it, says at the moment of tension between Voinitsky and his mother, "What a fine day. Not too hot." Uncle Vanya reples, "Yes, a fine day to hang oneself" (p. 184).

In act 2, the wind rattles the window and the sounds of the approaching storm alternate with the tapping of the night watchman, a sound that signifies the security of the household routine. Lightning strikes once, as the revelation of their destinies will later strike the participants. They begin to express their frustrations and their longings in various ways.

Serebryakov complains of being old and sick; Uncle Vanya laments his wasted life; Astrov (awakened by the storm) expresses his bohemianism by ordering Telegin to play his guitar when everyone is asleep and by asking for cognac. He also talks about beauty, and promises Sonya that he will never drink again. Sonya confesses her love for Astrov to Elena and Elena expresses her gathering frustration by wanting to play the piano: "I shall sit and play and cry, cry like a small child" (p. 200). But before she hears the answer of her husband, "It is forbidden," the pause is filled with another sound, that of the watchman, signaling the predominance of domestic routine over poetic longings. Elena tells him to stop his knock, but she herself is forbidden to express her own longings in the sounds of music. As Astrov says, "the storm passes us by, it only touched us by its tail." And so it does, except that the air is not cleared; it is heavy with unexpressed sounds.

In act 3, the storm moves inside. From act 1, which takes place in the afternoon, we move to the second act that takes place at night. In act 3, which will contain the central illumination, we are back in the daytime. At the beginning, Voinitsky announces the impending meeting at which the professor will make some kind of announcement. Yet before this announcement, which later elicits a violent reaction from Uncle Vanya, there is a scene that further motivates that response: Voinitsky sees Elena in Astrov's arms. A vision of his own happiness with Elena that had once been possible, together with the professor's ensuing speech concerning the sale of the estate, ignites Vanya's pathetic anger, although it resolves nothing.

As the Soviet critic, Ermilov noted, there is "a correlation of the final act with that earlier life on the estate, which existed here 'beyond the limits of the play,' even before Act One and the Serebryakovs' 'intrusion.' "[17] Every character says in his own way what Uncle Vanya said to the Professor: "All will be as before." Act 1 is set in the garden, an enclosed space. Act 4 takes place in Uncle Vanya's room, which is significantly both his bedroom and the office of the estate. All avenues of escape are obstructed; at the window stands a big table with account books, papers, and other objects that signify the estate. Both doors lead not outside but into some other enclosed spaces. The unexplored life is symbolized by a map of Africa hanging on the wall, which as Chekhov says is "apparently not needed by anyone here." It is an autumn evening and all is quiet. Thus the scene is set for the future arrival of winter, of death; it is recomposed "beyond the limits of the play."

The offer of a glass of tea which Astrov refused in the opening of the play is here again declined, but the glass of vodka refused earlier in the play is accepted. Astrov thus breaks his pledge to Sonya, but that was made in act 2 before the storm and the revelation that self-destruction was inevitable.

Right after Astrov accepts the vodka he begins talking as in the opening scene, but his subject matter is not his passing youth, nor generalizations about the trivial life. Rather, there follows a mundane conversation about his horse's lameness and the blacksmith. It is at this point that the famous remark about heat in Africa is made by Astrov. The existence of the faraway, sunny, unexplored continent is dismissed by a banal and meaningless remark: "I suppose it is terribly hot in Africa now." (p. 221). Probably it is in this same manner that the unexplored regions of their lives have also been dismissed. Those unknown regions with all their potentialities are not needed here, as the map itself is not needed. When Maksim Gorky saw *Uncle Vanya* he wrote to Chekhov:

In the last act of *Vanya* when after a long pause, the doctor speaks of the heat of Africa, I trembled with admiration of your talent and with fear for people and for our colorless wretched life. How magnificently you struck at the heart of things here, and how much to the point![18]

The routine has returned, and the predominant voices in this act are those concerned with routine: noodles, accounts, twenty pounds of oil, and Sonya's last speech that contains words like "bearing the trials that fate sends us," "humbly," "the long, long chain of days." Earthly dreams have finally been substituted by those that have nothing to do with life or people, those of skies alight with jewels and angels. There is a need to have faith. Against the familiar sounds of the night watchman, Telegin's guitar, and Mariya Vasilevna's scribbling in the margins of the book, Sonya's closing words, "We shall rest," (p. 223) sound like a death sentence.

V   Three Sisters

The success of *Uncle Vanya*, together with pressure from the Moscow Art Theatre for another play, prompted Chekhov to start serious work on *Three Sisters*. Chekhov labored over the manuscript from August to November of 1900, during which time he was very skeptical in his appraisal of its artistic merit. He was afraid that there were "a great many characters" and that it would "come out indistinct or pale." Tolstoi agreed with this appraisal of the play, complaining that "nothing happened" in it. After Chekhov visited Tolstoi in the Crimea during the winter of 1901 - 1902, he described the great artist's criticism of his plays as follows:

He was still confined to bed but talked a great deal about everything and about me, among other things. When eventually I get to my feet and make my farewells, he pulls me back by the arm, saying: "Kiss me!" and after giving me a kiss he suddenly bends over swiftly to my ear and says in that energetic quickfire old man's voice of his: "But I still can't stand your plays. Shakespeare's are terrible, but yours are even worse!"[19]

"Indistinct" and "pale" can hardly be applied to the final manuscript of *Three Sisters*. To begin with, Chekhov's innovative conception of dramatic structure differs radically from that of the traditional play with three or five acts that places the climax in the middle act. In contrast to this, Chekhov portrays the effects of passing time with an evenly balanced dramatic structure, in which the first two acts form a contrasting mirror to that which will follow.

The play begins in a spring that is full of hope for the three sisters, who have faith that they will return to Moscow before the fall. When the curtain goes up, Olga, Masha, and Irina are framed on stage alone together, but gradually the other major characters join them to celebrate the youngest sister Irina's name day. The tone is optimistic and it is clear that the sisters feel they will soon move to Moscow with their brother who they hope will become a university professor. The arrival of Vershinin, an old acquaintance from Moscow, further raises their spirits, acting as a link to them between the past and future. But at the beginning of act 2 these lighthearted feelings and hopes have been dispelled because of Andrei's unfortunate marriage to the vulgar, materialistic Natasha.

Significantly, the season is now winter, a time of sterility and barrenness, which is indeed the effect of Natasha's dominion over the household. In act 3 the season is not mentioned but there is a fire raging that is a symbolic representation of the destructive havoc being wreaked in the lives of the Prozorov sisters. The last act is set in autumn, which ironically recalls Irina's original prediction four years earlier that they would be settled in Moscow by the fall. The wide range of possibilities that life in Moscow represented has been permanently placed out of reach, and the sisters must adjust to the confines of a provincial existence.

Natasha, who in act 1 was a guest in the house, has now succeeded in evicting the sisters from the premises altogether. Natasha's final smug assertion of power over the sisters avenges her for her earlier position of servility to them. Natasha criticizes Irina's belt, which directly echoes Olga's admonition to her in the first act concerning the bright green belt she was wearing. However, although Natasha has attained material power, she has instilled neither

respect nor even fear in the sisters. In the end they remain spiritual-
ly unified as in the beginning by a faith in life and in the
possibilities of human nature. In the last scene Olga, Masha, and
Irina are framed together on the stage, mirroring the first representation of them in the play and underlining the fact that their
spiritual unity can not be destroyed by personal hardships.

The play is also united by imagery that runs throughout its four
acts. In the beginning of the play Irina says she feels as if she were
"sailing along, with a great blue sky above me and huge white birds
soaring about." Tuzenbakh responds by calling Irina his "little
white bird," and the association of a bird's freedom of migration
with Irina's desire to fly away to Moscow is thus implied. Tuzenbakh uses the image of a bird again in act 2, although this time the
context of his speech forms an ironic comment on Irina's feelings of
identity with a bird. In an argument with Vershinin, who argues for
faith in the future, Tuzenbakh responds with a metaphor that people are like migrating birds: to the unknowledgeable observer a
bird's flight might seem free, yet even these creatures are constantly
obeying laws of nature that bind them to pre-established patterns:

And life won't be any different, no, not only a couple of hundred years
from now, but a million. Life doesn't change, it always goes on the same; it
follows its own laws, which don't concern us and which we can't discover
anyway. Think of the birds flying South in the autumn, the cranes, for instance: they just fly on and on. It doesn't matter what they're thinking,
whether their heads are filled with great ideas or small ones, they just keep
flying, not knowing where or why. And they'll go on flying no matter how
many philosophers they happen to have flying with them. Let them
philosophize as much as they like, as long as they go on flying. (p. 250)

Irina will never reach Moscow because her life is governed by certain arbitrary laws of fate, and hence any identification of her with a
bird is tragically closer to this interpretation than the optimistic one
she originally conceived. In act 4 Chebutykin again compares Irina
to a bird, stressing that she is free of him because she can fly faster
than he:

CHEBUTYKIN, moved. My precious little girl, my dear child! You've gone
on so far ahead of me, I'll never catch up with you now. I've been left
behind like a bird that's too old and can't keep up with the rest of the flock.
Fly away, my dear, fly away, and God bless you! (p. 276)

Clothing imagery also unites this play. In the beginning Olga, the eldest, is wearing a blue school uniform, Masha a black dress, and Irina a white frock. These costumes are not only indicative of each woman's character, but also of their future fate. In act 4, after a lapse of four years, Olga is involved with teaching to the exclusion of everything else, Masha is mourning Vershinin's departure, and Irina is planning to be married. Nothing has changed.

The narrative technique employed by Chekhov is disjointed con versation between characters, which sometimes points to their isolation from one another, but which can also be used to develop a series of associations that are united subtextually. A good example of this device is given in the following lines:

MASHA But man has to have some faith, or at least he's got to seek it, otherwise his life will be empty . . . How can you live and not know why the cranes fly, why children are born, why the stars shine in the sky! . . . You must either know why you live, or else . . . nothing matters . . . everything's just nonsense and waste . . . *A pause.*

VERSHININ Yes, it's sad when one's youth has gone.

MASHA "It's a bore to be alive in this world, friends," that's what Gogol says.

TUSENBACH And I say: it's impossible to argue with you, friends! Let's drop the subject.

CHEBUTYKIN *reads out of the paper.* Balzac was married in Berditchev. (pp. 250 - 251)

Vershinin responds to Masha's generalizations about waste in a personal sense, commenting implicitly that, for them at least, only the timing of their meeting has blocked fulfillment. Masha responds with another generalization, that the course life takes is often boring, and at that moment Chebutykin comments that Balzac was married in Berdichev, which although seemingly unrelated to Masha's statement, serves as evidence of its veracity. This technique will later be used even more effectively in *The Cherry Orchard*.

Olga, Masha, and Irina are united by a longing for the excitement and love that is lacking in their lives, and to them Moscow is a sort of "earthly paradise." As the other characters are introduced, it is revealed that they too are searching for fulfillment in life: whether it be of the most base, materialistic sort, as in the case of Natasha, or the most abstract form of a "dream for mankind," in the case of Vershinin. Masha and Vershinin are the most idealistic characters in *Three Sisters*. The lyrical mood associated with Masha is first developed with her recitation of the first two lines from Pushkin's *Ruslan and Ludmila:* "A green oak grows by a curving shore,/And round that hangs a golden chain." Masha's melancholy longing for beauty and for a more poetic life finds its echo in Vershinin's abstract vision of the future:

Why in two or three hundred years life on this earth will be wonderfully beautiful. Man longs for a life like that, and if he doesn't have it right now he must imagine it, wait for it, dream about it, prepare for it: he must know more and see more than his father or his grandfather did. (Act 1, p. 237)

A love affair develops between the two of them despite the fact that they are both married and that their ephemeral, lyrical happiness will have the same doomed fate as all their dreams. Masha and Vershinin's love has a fairy-tale quality, and they often communicative with snatches from a melody which expresses the poetic quality of their feelings for one another.

The youngest sister, Irina, also longs for a different sort of life, which will be enobled by meaningful work and beautified by a passionate love. She feels sure that fulfillment awaits her in Moscow, if only she could break away from the dreary provincial town which binds her to a boring, mechanical job and to relationships with men to whom she is indifferent.

Three men are in love with Irina: the elderly Dr. Chebutykin, the young profligate Soleny, and the dependable but unexciting Count Tuzenbakh. Dr. Chebutykin was once the unsuccessful suitor of Irina's mother, and he has transferred his unrequited affections to her. The inappropriate and slightly unpleasant quality of the doctor's attachment to Irina are underlined by two symbols that draw attention to his ignorance and to his old age. The samovar that Chebutykin presents to Irina on her twentieth birthday is the traditional gift for a silver wedding anniversary, and it causes consternation among the sisters rather than pleasure. Later, the doctor breaks the clock that belonged to Irina's mother, symbolizing his desire to erase time and also his carelessness toward other people's deepest feelings. Chebutykin's constant reading of the newspaper and quoting of trifles from it draws attention to the poverty of his mind, and again to his old age.

Irina's other unsuccessful suitor, Soleny, is much more dangerous and evil than the doctor. Whereas the doctor is indifferent to those around him, Soleny views himself as a second Lermontov, who has the right to harm others. When Irina refuses to return his love, he tells her that she shall have no successful suitors, and determines to kill Tuzenbakh. Soleny is identified with the animal violences of a bear from the beginning of the play. He attempts to defend himself against Masha's just criticism of him in the first act with lines from Krylov's fable: "He had hardly time to catch his breath, Before the bear was hugging him to death." However, it is clear in the last act that Soleny himself is the bear, and Tuzenbakh his victim. Before accompanying Soleny to the duel, Chebutykin recites these same lines back to Soleny, making the identification absolutely clear. Another symbol that delineates Soleny's character is the bottle of scent which he constantly sprinkles over his hands and chest, an act which indicates his desire to expiate himself from guilt.

Like the three sisters, their brother Andrei is a refined idealist who dreams of becoming one day a professor at Moscow University. He is constantly associated with his violin and with the books he reads even after all hope for an academic career has vanished. Andrei is the victim of his own inaction, as well as of his coarse wife Natasha and her lover Protopopov. Natasha is a woman with neither refinement nor kindness, who is interested only in advancing her material position in life. After her marriage to Andrei, she exercises despotic control over the household, makes a cuckold of her husband, and finally evicts the three sisters from their own house althogether. A lighted candle, symbolizing destructive fire, becomes Natasha's leitmotif as she gradually gains more power. Although her lover Protopopov never appears on the stage, it is clear that this influence is likewise evil. Masha's initial mistrust of Protopopov and her association of him with the bear of Russian folklore prove to be well founded.

Three Sisters further develops the theme of the meaning of human life which was broached by Sonya at the end of *Uncle Vanya*. The only two characters in the play who are not philosophically inclined, Natasha and Protopopov, are those who are shortsighted enough to triumph in temporal power relationships. All the other characters are in some way caught in a web of dreams that makes them more ineffectual in life than they might otherwise be.

In the end, all these characters must adjust to the frustrations of life in some way: for the doctor it is with indifference, for Andrei it is with resignation, and for Soleny it is with violence. Irina, Olga, and Masha must abandon their dreams of going to Moscow and must also deal with life as it is. At the end of the play Irina again speaks of work, and Masha and Olga advocate devoting themselves to improving life for future generations. There is a dignity in the three sisters' struggle to create meaning in life after it has been stripped of their most beautiful illusions, which makes this Chekhov's most serious play. It is a drama with comic elements rather than vice versa.

VI   The Cherry Orchard

After the success of *Three Sisters* in Yalta, Chekhov wanted to write another play that he said would be a joyful comedy. He wrote to his wife on March 7, 1901: "The next play I am going to write will be funny, very funny, at least in conception."[20]

Chekhov took two years to write *The Cherry Orchard*. Perhaps his illness slowed his pace, or maybe he sensed that this would be his last major work, and he wanted to make it a masterpiece. At any rate, while Chekhov was writing *The Cherry Orchard* he surrounded it with an aura of mystery that indicates his own very personal attitude toward the play. By the summer of 1902, Chekhov still had not told anyone the title of his forthcoming play, and it was only to comfort his ill wife that he told her and she was the first to know. "Do you want me to tell you the name of my new play?"[21] he asked her. Olga later recalled that even though they were alone in the room, Chekhov would not say the title out loud, but whispered it to her.

Apparently the prototypes that would later be developed into the characters of *The Cherry Orchard* were in Chekhov's mind for some time. When he was in Europe in 1901, Chekhov wrote his wife about the Russian women living a dissipated life there, and singled out Monte Carlo as a representative city. Originally, Ranevskaya was designated in Chekhov's notebooks as just such an elderly Russian woman. Chekhov also told Stanislavsky about a Russian landowner who stayed in bed all day if he was not dressed by his servant: an obvious exaggeration of Gaev's passive personality. Several people whom Chekhov knew had Epikhodov's qualities, although each of his friends thought they recognized someone else in this figure. Sharlotta was modeled on an English governess who was Chekhov's neighbor; although to that woman's cheerful, good-humored, and eccentric nature, Chekhov added a dimension of loneliness and alienation.

Chekhov considered Varya as "a fool, but a kind fool." He thought of Lopakhin as perhaps being the main character, and designated this role for Stanislavsky right from the beginning. Chekhov did not conceive of Lopakhin as simply a vulgar representative of capitalism and the new bourgeois class. He made the point in one of his letters that a serious, pious girl like Vavara couldn't have fallen in love with Lopakhin as she did if he were just an insensitive merchant.

When *The Cherry Orchard* was first produced on January 17, 1904, it was not greeted as a success. Some complained that "nothing happened," others remarked that the theme of the decaying landowning class was already exhausted by playwright Alexander Ostrovsky. These criticisms totally overlooked Chekhov's intention to address the audience on the subtextual level of unconscious sensibility, rather than on that of surface dramatic action.

Francis Fergussen sees the four acts of *The Cherry Orchard* in classical terms.[22] He identifies the first act as the prologue (the stating of necessary facts: in this case the cherry orchard's imminent scale); the second act as the agon (the conflict of characters in a drama: here between the values the characters attach to the cherry orchard and their efforts to save it); the third act as the peripety (when the cherry orchard is sold and the fact is announced at the party); and the fourth act as the epiphany, or completion of action, which occurs when the characters must accept the loss of the cherry orchard.

The plot structure is not nearly as meaningful as the impact of events on the inner sensibilities of the characters. The loss of the cherry orchard serves as a catalyst that elicits revealing responses from each of the characters.

Mrs. Ranevskaya and her brother Gaev are totally without practical ability, yet both pride themselves on their refinement and appreciation of beauty. Neither of them is capable of acting like a merchant, and thus even as their world crumbles beneath them they continue to uphold the same values. Lyubov squanders her remaining money on luxuries, and Gaev insulates himself from the world by playing an imaginary game of billiards. Likewise, the old servant Firs makes the cherry orchard an inviolable aesthetic symbol of the traditional order. He fondly remembers days of prosperity when the sale of the sweet dark cherries yielded enough income to support the entire estate in splendor. However, these memories will die with Firs' generation, and offer no philosophy to the young people in the play.

Trofimov and Anya have adopted a more impersonal and optimistic view of the cherry orchard's loss. The student Trofimov
argues at the end of act 2 that "The whole of Russia is our orchard.
The earth is great and beautiful and there are many wonderful
places in it" (p. 316). Trofimov and Anya thus view the loss of the
orchard as the inevitable and positive redistribution of resources
from a privileged class to the whole Russian people. However, the
irony will be that the profiteering merchant Lopakhin rather than
"the people" will benefit from the sale of the property and that,
furthermore, his plans for "development" will destroy its beauty.

Character portraits are further developed by the parodies that exist between the gentry and their servants. Sharlotta's lack of identity
and her ludicrous behavior are a satirical reflection of Ranevskaya.
Dunyasha is a parody of the whole idea of the delicate young
noblewoman. Epikhodov with his twenty-two miseries is a parody of
Gaev, as too is the "spoiled" Yasha, who insists "How uncivilized
this country is."

Yasha's coarse words to Firs, "Nadoel ty ded, xot' by ty skoree
podox" ("How you bore me, old man. Why don't you just go away
and die. It's about time.") (p. 325), are a parody of the irresponsible
attitude which Ranevskaya, Varya, Gaev, Anya, and Trofimov later
show toward the old servant. Although they wouldn't be capable of
consciously sharing Yasha's cruel attitude, at the end of the play,
not one member of the family is concerned enough to ascertain that
Firs has actually been sent to the hospital, and he is left alone to
die.

The characters are also depicted through Chekhov's astute
description of their speech peculiarities. Ranevskaya's dialogue is
composed of emotional, sentimental, and at times melodramatic ex-
pressions which convey her helplessness. Such lines as: "I dream,"
I'll die," "Have pity on me, my darling table"; and the repetition of
the phrases "Perhaps it would be good to," "I don't know what to
think," and "I'm expecting something" underline her feeling of insecurity. On the other hand, Ranevskaya's warmhearted nature is
expressed in her speech by the constant use of endearing terms. She
often addresses people as "my darling, my friend, my dear," and
repeats these words tenderly.

Gaev's speech is at times prosaic, repetitive, and empty of meaning. His diversion of imaginary billiards is a defense against reality
which preoccupies and soothes his mind, and it is highly fitting that
he always seems to be sucking a gumdrop as he describes fictive

games. However, Gaev is sentimental, and he periodically pronounces lyrical apostrophes to the past, to nature, and even to an old bookcase he is fond of. Although these oratorical speeches are scorned by the younger generation, there is much truth in them, especially in his declamation to nature:

Oh nature, glorious nature, shining with eternal light, so beautiful and indifferent . . . you whom we call Mother, you unite within yourself both life and death, you create and you destroy . . . . (pp. 314 - 315)

Lopakhin's speech is predominantly practical, although folk words such as *nebos'*, *prorva*, and *ob tu poru* intrude into his conversation. He often refers to numbers, and his vulgarity is reflected in his use of such words as "pig," "idiot," *baba*, and *bolvan*. On the one occasion that Lopakhin quotes from *Hamlet* his lack of education is further evident in the error, "Okhmeliya, get thee to a monastery!" (p. 316)

The student Trofimov's speech is educated and refined, and it is filled with imagery and metaphors. Like Vershinin, Trofimov has faith in the future, and his words to Anya are reminiscent of those spoken to Masha in *Three Sisters:*

To free ourselves of all that is petty and ephemeral, all that prevents us from being free and happy, that's the whole aim and meaing of our life. Forward! We march forward irresistibly toward that bright star that shines there in the distance. Forward! Don't fall behind, friends! (p. 316)

Trofimov's effeminate appearance and his rationalization of celibacy with the line, "We are higher than love" (p. 322) render him comic. In act 3 he chides Ranevskaya for not being able to accept the truth about her lover, yet he himself can't face the implications of the fact that he has never had a mistress.

These very peculiarities which are so important to Chekhov's characterization do not serve the plot but rather play a vital role in the development of the play's comedy. Each character's idiosyncrasies are amusing in themselves, and everybody is preoccupied with his own subjective view to the point that communication becomes comic. Conversations have the quality of a mosaic, and the juxtaposition of phrases is artistically arranged to underline the absurd tragedy of human isolation. The following passages serve to illustrate this point:

Lyubov: The nursery!
Varya: How cold it is! My hands are numb! [To Lyubov]
  Your rooms are the same as always . . .
Lyubov: The nursery, my dear, beautiful room! . . .
Gaev: The train was two hours late. Just think of it!
  Such efficiency!
Sharlotta: And my dog eats nuts, too. (p. 292)

Firs: I've lived for a long time. They were planning to marry me before
your father was born . . . I remember everyone was happy at that
time . . .
Lopakhin: That was the good life all right! All the peasants were flogged.
Firs: [not having heard him] That's right! The peasants belonged to their
masters, and the masters belonged to the peasants; but now everything's all
confused.
Gaev: Be quiet, Firs. Tomorrow I've got to go to town . . . (p. 312)

The use of symbolism is as important in this play as in *Three
Sisters*. The significance of the cherry orchard itself has already
been discussed. The color white is used to draw attention to the
purity and beauty of Gaev's and Lyubov's past. In act 1 Varya mentions that one of Lyubov's favorite rooms is white (p. 292), and later
when they look out at the orchard Gaev and Lyubov remark upon
its whiteness, imagining their mother among the trees (p. 301). Firs,
who lives according to the old traditions, is often dressed in a white
waistcoat, and on one occasion he is wearing white gloves. Varya is
constantly carrying a ring of keys, which draws attention to her
position of practical authority in the house. At the end of the third
act, when Lopakhin announces that he has bought the orchard, she
flings these keys at him.

The most important symbol in *The Cherry Orchard* is the breaking string that is sounded first near the end of act 2, and then again
at the end of the play. In his book *The Breaking String*, Maurice
Valency says of it:

The symbol is broad; it would be folly to try to assign to it a more precise
meaning than the author chose to give it. But its quality is not equivocal.
Whatever of sadness remains unexpressed in *The Cherry Orchard*, this
sound expresses.[23]

Valency adds that the breaking string is associated with the
melancholy of a passing generation. He notes that in act 2 it is
heard after Gaev's apostrophe to nature has been rejected by the

young people listening to him, and again at the end of the play, after Firs has been abandoned.

The melancholy fatalism that is a constant undercurrent in *The Cherry Orchard* enlarges the scope of its comedy. It is not a funny play in the traditional sense of the word, but rather in the framework of a more conscious, modern concept of humor of Henri Bergson's conception. The isolation that every human being lives in, the passing of time, and the imminence of death are cosmic tragedies. Only a great artist such as Chekhov could succeed in portraying the comic aspects of metaphysical questions which have been plaguing man for centuries.

VII *Epilogue*

In the recollections of those who were professionally involved with Chekhov's creations, actors and directors, the playwright emerges in the same light as the author of short stories who is able to zero in on a small part to reveal the whole.

"When we asked him," writes Olga Knipper, describing the actors' interaction with Chekhov, "he replied suddenly, as though not to the point, as though he was speaking in general and we did not know whether to interpret his remark seriously or in jest. But it seemed so only in the first minute, and then instantly we sensed that this remark, seemingly uttered in passing, began to penetrate the brain, the soul, and from a barely perceptible human character trait all the essence of Man began to emerge."[29]

K. Stanislavsky recalls that when he first played Trigorin in *The Seagull*, Chekhov praised his acting ability highly yet added that "but it isn't my character. I didn't write that."

To Stanislavsky's question in what did he err, Chekhov replied, "He has checkered pants and his shoes have holes in them." And he refused to elaborate.

"And he always made his remarks in this manner, briefly and imagistically. They surprised one and remained in one's memory. It was as though A. P. gave us charades from which it was impossible to rid oneself until one could fathom them."[25]

"I deciphered this charade only six years later," writes Stanislavsky, "when we performed *Seagull* again."

Stanislavsky says that even when he directed one of Chekhov's plays for the hundredth time he never failed to discover something new in the well-known text and in the well-known feelings evoked by the play.[26]

It is this immeasurable depth of a writer that affords his readers the joy of perpetual discovery and that makes Chekhov alive today, the only immortality to which he would aspire.

Notes and References

Chapter One

1. A. P. Chekhov, *Sobranie sochinenii v dvenadtsati tomakh*, vol. 12, entitled *Pis'ma* (Letters) (Moscow, 1950), p. 120 (Letter to Aleksei Suvorin).
2. Ibid.
3. Avrahm Yarmolinsky, *Letters of Anton Chekhov* (New York, 1973), p. 28.
4. Ernest Simmons, *Chekhov: A Biography* (Boston, 1962), p. 118.
5. *Pis'ma*, vol. 12, p. 128.
6. Ibid., p. 187.
7. Simmons, *Chekhov*, p. 240.
8. *Pis'ma*, vol. 12, p. 203.
9. Simmons, *Chekhov*, p. 243.
10. Ibid., p. 326.
11. N. I. Gitovich, *Letopis' zhizni i tvorchestva A. P. Chekhova*, (Moscow, 1955) p. 433.
12. Simmons, *Chekhov*, p. 418.
13. *Pis'ma*, vol. 12, p. 281.
14. Ibid., p. 282.
15. Simmons, *Chekhov*, p. 451.
16. Ibid.
17. Yarmolinsky, *Letters of Anton Chekhov*, p. 371.
18. N. I. Gitovich, and I. V. Fedorova, *A. P. Chekhov v vospominaniakh sovremennikov* (Moscow, 1960), p. 701.

Chapter Two

1. A. P. Chekhov, *Sobranie sochinenie*, Izdatel 'stvo Pravda, Moskva, 1950. Chapter and page references in text refer to this edition, unless otherwise stated.
2. N. I. Gitovich, *Letopis' zhizni i tvorchestva Chekhova*, p. 52.
3. Berdnikov, *A. P. Chekhov*, pp. 31 - 32.

Chapter Three

1. Quoted in Ernest J. Simmons, *Chekhov*, p. 96.
2. Ibid., p. 96.
3. *Pis'ma*, vol. 12, p. 32.
4. A. N. Vasil'eva, *Stilisticheskii analiz iazyka* (Moscow, 1966), pp. 35-49.

5. Ibid., p. 40.
6. *Pis'ma*, vol. 2 (Moscow, 1975), p. 166.
7. *Pis'ma*, vol. 12, p. 74.
8. Quoted in Simmons, *Chekhov*, p. 118.
9. *Pis'ma*, vol. 12, p. 76
10. Quoted in Nils Ake Nilsson, *Studies in Čechov's Narrative Technique*, p. 26.
11. V. Shklovsky, *Zametki o proze russkikh klassikov* (Moscow, 1955), p. 428 - 29.
12. *Dead Souls:* the edition published by Norton (New York, 1971) is referred to in these instances.
13. *Pis'ma*, vol. 12, p. 88.
14. Ibid., p. 90.

Chapter Four

1. Gitovich, *Letopis'zhizni i tvorchestva A. P. Chekhova* (Moscow, 1955), p. 259 - 260.
2. *Pis'ma*, vol. 12, pp. 200 - 201.
3. Ibid., p. 110.
4. Ibid., p. 136.
5. Ibid., p. 139.
6. Ibid., p. 143.
7. Mikhail Lermontov, *A Hero of Our Times*, trans. Nabokov (New York, 1958), p. 161.
8. Ibid., p. 162.
9. *Pis'ma*, vol. 12, p. 223.
10. Ibid., pp. 235 - 236.
11. A. Skaftymov, *Stat'i o russkoi literature*, Saratovskoe knizhnoe izdat, 1958, p. 301.

Chapter Five

1. Avrahm Yarmolinsky, *Letters of Anton Chekhov* (New York, 1973), p. 204.
2. Ibid., p. 223.
3. Ibid., p. 319.
4. Ermilov, *A. P. Chekhov* (Moskva, 1953), p. 347.
5. Ibid., p. 348.
6. Ibid., pp. 348 - 350.
7. Berdnikov, *A. P. Chekhov*, p. 401.

Chapter Six

1. Berdnikov, *A. P. Chekhov*, p. 433.
2. Tolstoi, "Krug Chteniia" in *Polnoe sobranie sochinenii* (Moskva, 1957), Vol. 51, p. 375.

3. Poggioli, "Storytelling in a Double Key" in *The Phoenix and the Spider* (Cambridge, Mass., 1957), pp. 109 - 131.

4. Ibid., p. 122.

5. Thomas Winner, *Chekhov and His Prose* (New York, 1966), pp. 210 - 216. See also Karl Kramer, *The Chameleon and the Dream* (Mouton, The Hague, 1970), pp. 161 - 162.

6. *Chekhov-Gorki perepiska, stat'i i vyskazyvaniia* (N. Gosizd, 1951), p. 6.

7. Nilsson (Stockholm, 1968), pp. 62 - 84.

8. Ibid., pp. 105 - 109.

9. Ibid., p. 67.

10. Papernyi, *A. P. Chekhov* (Moskva, 1960), p. 284.

Chapter Seven

1. A. P. Chekhov, Polnoe sobranie sochinenii i pisem, vol. 12 (Moskva, 1949). In this edition the play appears as *P'esa bez nazvanija* (A Play without a title). All references are to this edition, pp. 7 - 165.

2. *Pis'ma*, vol. 12, p. 58.

3. Ibid., p. 117.

4. Ibid., p. 116.

5. *Six Plays of Chekhov.* New England versions and introduction by Robert W. Corrigan (New York, 1962). All of the following page references to Chekhov's plays refer to this edition.

6. *Pis'ma*, vol. 12, p. 120.

7. Ibid., p. 58.

8. Gitovich N. I. Letopis' Zhizni Chekhova, p. 245.

9. Ibid., p. 246.

10. Yarmolinsky, *Letters,* p. 353.

11. *Pis'ma*, vol. 12, p. 248.

12. Yarmolinsky, *Letters,* p. 209.

13. Ibid., p. 319.

14. *Russkie vedomosti*, 1899, No. 298.

15. Quoted in *Chekhov* by Ernest J. Simmons (Boston, 1962), p. 495.

16. *Pis'ma*, vol. 12, p. 311.

17. Ermilov, "*Uncle Vanya:* The Play's Movement," in *Chekhov: A Collection of Critical Essays,* ed. R. L. Jackson (Englewood Cliffs, N.J., 1967), p. 119.

18. M. g. A. Ch., *Perepiska, stat'i, vyskazyvaniia,* (M-L, 1937), p. 11.

19. Recalled by Bunin, *Chekhov* "Vospominanlay I. A. Bunina" in *Chekhov* Literature Nashedstuo, vol. 68 (Moscow, 1960) p. 660.

20. A. I. Reviakin, *Vishnevyi Sad A. P. Chekhova* (Moskva, 1960), p. 43.

21. Ibid., pp. 45 - 46.

22. Francis Fergussen, *The Idea of a Theater* (Princeton, N.J., 1949), p. 163.

23. Valency, *The Breaking String* (New York, 1966), p. 287.

24. Olga Knipper, *A. P. Chekhov v vospominaniiah sovremennikov* (Moskva, 1960), p. 686.

25. Ibid., pp. 379 - 380.

26. Ibid., p. 397.

Selected Bibliography

PRIMARY SOURCES

In Russian:
Chekhov, A. P. *Sorbranie sochinenii v dvenadtsati tomakh.* Moskva: Pravda, 1950.

In English:
Chekhov Plays. Translated by Elisaveta Fen. Harmondsworth: Penguin, 1951.
Lady with Lapdog and Other Stories. Translated by David Magarshack. Harmondsworth: Penguin, 1964.
The Plays of Tchehov. Translated by Constance Garnett. 2 vols. London: Chatto & Windus, 1922 - 23 (reprinted 1965 - 70).
The Portable Chekhov. Translated by Avrahm Yarmolinsky. New York: Viking, 1965.
Selected Stories. Translated by Ann Dunnigan. New York: New American Library, 1965.
Six Plays of Chekhov. New English versions and introduction by Robert W. Corrigan. Holt, Rinehart and Winston, New York, 1962.
Stories 1889 - 1891. Translated by Ronald Hingley. ("The Oxford Chekhov," vol. V) London: Oxford University Press, 1965.
Stories 1895 - 1897. Translated by Ronald Hingley. ("The Oxford Chekhov," vol. VIII) London: Oxford University Press, 1965.
The Tales of Tchehov. Translated by Constance Garnett. 13 vols. London: Chatto & Windus, 1916 - 23.
Tchekov's Plays and Stories. Translated by S. S. Koteliansky. London: Everyman, 1937.
Ward No. 6 and Other Stories. Translated by Ann Dunnigan. New York: New American Library, 1965.

SECONDARY SOURCES

In Russian:
BERDNIKOV, G. A. *P. Chekhov.* Moskva-Leningrad: 1961. An attempt to find Chekhov the ideologist-philosopher and to trace the development of his ideas as well as his craft.
Chekhov dramaturg. Moskva-Leningrad: Gos-izdatel'stvo iskusstva, 1957. As the title indicates, it is a study of Chekhov as a playwright. Analysis of plays in chronological order.

161

CHUDAKOV, A. P. *Poetika Chekhova*. Moskva: 1971. Divides Chekhov's work into three periods. Deals with the narrative structure. Examines Chekhov's work in comparison with his predecessors.

DERMAN, A. *Tvorcheskii portret Chekhova*. Moskva: 1929. A concise analysis of Chekhov's development as a man and as an artist. Many interesting insights into his "Disharmony" and how it affected his art.

ERMILOV, V. *Anton Pavlovich Chekhov: 1860 - 1904*. Moskva: Gosizdatel'stvo khudozhestvennoi literatury, 1953. General commentary on Chekhov's stories and plays with biographical information. Gives an outline of his development as a writer.

PAPERNYI, Z. *A. P. Chekhov: ocherk tvorchestva*. Moskva: 1960. Traces the most important parts of his development as a writer. Deals only with stories.

In English:

BRUFORD, W. H. *Anton Chekhov*. Studies in Modern Literature and Thought. New Haven: Yale University Press, 1957. A general outline of his development as an artist.
Chekhov and His Russia. Hamden, Ct.: Archon Books, 1971. An attempt to present Russia through Chekhov's eyes and to relate Chekhov to his national background.

EEKMAN, T. (ed.) *Anton Čexov, 1860 - 1960: Some Essays*. Leiden: E. J. Brill, 1960. Twenty essays dealing with Chekhov's craft and some biographical information.

GILLES, DANIEL. *Chekhov: Observer Without Illusion*. Translated by Charles Lam Markmann. New York: Funk and Wagnal, 1968. Interpretive biography, examines Chekhov's relationship with different women. Discusses plays.

HAHN, BEVERLY. *Chekhov: a study of major stories and plays*. New York: Cambridge University Press, 1977. This study begins with the examination of *The Cherry Orchard* as an introduction and then reverts to his early work. Sound analysis on some of his major works, and an especially interesting examination of his relationship with Tolstoi, as well as a chapter on the women in his fiction.

HINGLEY, RONALD. *Chekhov: a biographical and critical study*. London: Unwin Books, 1966. An attempt to present both his life and his work. Some observations on Chekhov's language, simplicity, and restraint, as well as on his attitude toward Russia and the issues of his time.

JACKSON, ROBERT (ed.). *Chekhov: A Collection of Critical Essays*. Englewood, N.J.: Prentice-Hall, 1967.

KRAMER, KARL D. *The Chameleon and the Dream: The Image of Reality in Cexov's Stories*. Slavistic Printings and Reprintings, 78. The Hague, Mouton, 1970. Deals with some major themes of Chekhov's stories.

MAGARSHACK, DAVID. *Chekhov the Dramatist*. London: 1952. Useful in studying Chekhov's plays. Divides his plays into those of direct and indirect action.

PITCHER, HARVEY. *The Chekov Play: A New Interpretation.* New York: Barnes & Noble, 1973. As the title suggests, an innovative interpretation of his four major plays.

RAYFIELD, DONALD. *Chekhov: The Evolution of His Art.* London: Paul Elek, 1975. General study of his work, sound scholarship with biographical information.

SIMMONS, ERNEST J. *Chekhov: A Biography.* Boston: Little, Brown & Co., 1962. A detailed biography that lacks analysis but presents a complete and popularized chronicle of Chekhov's life.

SPEIRS, LOGAN. *Tolstoy and Chekhov.* New York: Cambridge University Press, 1972. A comparative study of two writers. A search for common themes and concerns.

STYAN, J. L. *Chekhov in Performance: A Commentary to His Major Plays.* New York: Cambridge University Press, 1971. A study of Chekhov's plays exclusively.

VALENCY, MAURICE. *The Breaking String: The Plays of Anton Chekhov.* New York: Oxford University Press, 1966. Studies Chekhov's plays in relation to the drama of the West and Russia.

WINNER, THOMAS. *Chekhov and His Prose.* New York: Holt, Rinehart and Winston, 1966. Examines Chekhov's stories and makes comments on their style and content.

Life and Letters:

Anton Chekhov's Life and Thought: Selected Letters and Commentary. Translated by Michael Henry Heim in collaboration with Simon Karlinsky. Selection, introduction, and commentary by Simon Karlinsky. Berkeley: University of California Press, 1975, xiv, 494. The lengthy introduction, copious notes together with the selected letters form a critical biography of Chekhov.

CHEKHOV, ANTON. *Letters of Anton Chekhov.* Translated by A. Yarmolinsky, Bernard Guilbert Guerney, and Lynn Solotaroff. New York: Viking Press, 1973. Over 400 letters in chronological order. Detailed index. The best collection of letters in English.

Index